NON OBVIOUS

How To Think Different, Curate Ideas & Predict The Future

ROHIT BHARGAVA

Best Selling Author of *Likeonomics*

IDEAPRESS
PUBLISHING

IDEAPRESS
PUBLISHING

Copyright ©2015 by Rohit Bhargava

All rights reserved.

Published in the United States by IdeaPress Publishing.

IDEAPRESS PUBLISHING
www.ideapresspublishing.com

All trademarks are the property of their respective companies.

Cover Design by Jeff Miller/Faceout Studios
Cover Photo by Javier Pérez

Cataloging-in-Publication Data is on file with the Library of Congress.

ISBN: 978-1-940858-10-4
ISBN: 978-1-940858-11-1 (ebook)

PROUDLY PRINTED IN THE UNITED STATES OF AMERICA
By Selby Marketing Associates

SPECIAL SALES
IdeaPress Books are available at a special discount for bulk purchases for
sales promotions and premiums, or for use in corporate training programs.
Special editions, including personalized covers, custom forewords, corporate
imprints and bonus content are also available. For more details, email
info@ideapresspublishing.com or contact the author directly.

*No animals were harmed in the writing, printing or distribution of this book.
The trees, unfortunately, were not so lucky.*

NON OBVIOUS

*To my parents – for always giving me
a chance to see the world in my own way …
even if it wasn't always non-obvious.*

business owners, entrepreneurs, heads of marketing, and CEOs have struggled with for years —how do you identify where the market is headed and be there first, ready to take advantage of it. Artfully lacing stories together to pull out simple, yet powerful trends, Rohit offers a blueprint for making trend identification a key component of your business strategy. The format of his book makes it easy for the novice to adopt these principles, and for the expert to glean pearls of wisdom. While the title is Non Obvious, your next step should be obvious —read this book today!

—JOEY COLEMAN
Chief Experience Composer at Design Symphony

"Lots of books tell you to "think different" but *Non-Obvious* is one of the few books that actually teaches you how to do it. Whether you are trying to persuade clients, motivate a team, or just impress a demanding boss —*Non-Obvious* can help you succeed. I've already purchased copies for my entire team."

—JOHN GERZEMA
New York Times best-selling author and social strategist

"Very few people understand the world of digital business better than Rohit and I have introduced my clients to his ideas for years. His new book is a must-read resource for learning to see patterns, anticipate global trends, and think like a futurist every day!"

—GERD LEONHARD
Author and Keynote Speaker Basel / Switzerland

"It doesn't take a crystal ball to predict that digital is the future. Rather than tell you what you already know, Rohit sets his sights on something much more important: helping you adopt a more curious and observant mindset to understand the world around you. If you believe in a lifetime of learning, read this book!"

—JONATHAN BECHER
Chief Marketing Officer, SAP

"In *Non-Obvious* Rohit shares valuable tips, tricks, methodologies and insightful curated trends to help readers navigate the future. Recommended!"

—ROSS DAWSON
Chairman, Future Exploration Network

"*Non-Obvious* is a powerhouse 'must read' for corporate executives, marketeers and product and service developers. Rohit Bhargava provides valuable, entertaining and easily understood sideways insights into critical trends shaping the near future. He lifts the lid on the myths surrounding the dark arts of trend prediction and offers very practical guidance on how to spot, curate and capitalize on Non Obvious trends."

—ROHIT TALWAR
Global Futurist and CEO Fast Future Research

"The best books approach their topic with a spirit of generosity. Rohit's new book offers insight into the business and cultural trends that matter. And why they do. And what actions they might inspire. But more than that, it also generously teaches you how to develop your own process, for evaluating the trends that matter and those that don't. Also, it's well-written. Which makes it a joy (and not a chore!) to read!"

—ANN HANDLEY
Chief Content Officer, MarketingProfs

"A lot of books promise to help you see things differently but Rohit's book actually delivers. His insightful blend of visual thinking and business strategy shows you how to find meaningful patterns that others miss. A real mind-opener."

—SUNNI BROWN
Author, *Gamestorming* and *The Doodle Revolution*

EARLY PRAISE FOR *NON-OBVIOUS*

"*Non-Obvious* is a sharp, articulate, and immediately useful book about one of my favorite topics: the future. Filled with actionable advice and entertaining stories, Rohit offers an essential guidebook to using the power of curation to understand and prepare for the future of business."

—DANIEL H. PINK
Author of *To Sell Is Human* and *Drive*

"Shatter your magic crystal ball, and toss out the tea leaves. In this book, Rohit shows us how and where to find the future trends that will shape your business, your brand, and even your own decision-making."

—SALLY HOGSHEAD
NY Times bestselling author of *How The World Sees You*

"There are very few books that I read hoping that no one else around me will. They're the books that are so insightful, so thought provoking and so illuminating that they provide powerful competitive advantage. *Non-Obvious* is one of those. Pass on it at your own peril."

—SHIV SINGH
SVP Global Head of Digital & Marketing Transformation at VISA
and author of *Social Media Marketing For Dummies*

"*Non-Obvious* should be called *oblivious* since that's how you'll be if this book isn't on your shelf. I actually wish some of Rohit's predictions won't come true ('Selfie Confidence'!? Nooo!) ... but usually they do. He's the best at this, and this book shows you why."

—SCOTT STRATTEN
Four time Best-Selling Author, including 2014 Sales Book of the Year: *UnSelling*

"This is one of those rare books that delivers insights that are both useful and help illuminate where business is going. It's a great read."

—CHARLES DUHIGG
Author of the bestseller *The Power Of Habit*

"For the last four years, Rohit has helped make the non-obvious obvious by spotlighting trends to help anyone prepare their business for the future. It gets better every year so if you haven't been reading, it's time to start."

—RYAN HOLIDAY
Author of *Trust Me I'm Lying* and *Growth Hacker Marketing*

"The aim of many business books is to give a man a fish. Rohit generously goes one better—not by simply telling us what's working, but by showing us how to apply his thinking for ourselves."

—BERNADETTE JIWA
Bestselling author, award-winning blogger & keynote speaker

"Rohit Bhargava's "Likeonomics" is the gold standard on understanding the social economy. His new book had me at "predict the future" but there's much more than that in here. It's about seeing the world in a new way — plus a powerful argument for how curation can change your organization."

—SREE SREENIVASAN
Chief Digital Officer, The Metropolitan Museum of Art Host,
"@Sree Show" podcast on CBS @Playit network

"Rohit provides a goldmine of ideas and trends that will shape the future of marketing and product development. Read this book to get in front of the herd."

—GUY KAWASAKI
Chief Evangelist of Canva
Author of *The Art of the Start, 2.0*

"Seeing things that others don't is perhaps the highest form of creativity that exists. Unlock the Non-Obvious approach and you can write your ticket to success in any field."

—JOHN JANTSCH
Author of *Duct Tape Marketing* and *Duct Tape Selling*

Rohit Bhargava collects ideas the way frequent fliers collect miles. His infectious enthusiasm for trends and strategy is a recipe for success for your enterprise. In *Non Obvious*, he provides the solution to a problem

CONTENTS

———

PART I
THE ART OF CURATING TRENDS

PART II
THE 2015 NON-OBVIOUS TREND REPORT

CULTURE & CONSUMER BEHAVIOR TRENDS

MARKETING & SOCIAL MEDIA TRENDS

MEDIA & EDUCATION TRENDS

TECHNOLOGY & DESIGN TRENDS

PART III
THE TREND ACTION GUIDE

APPENDICES: THE PAST YEARS' NON-OBVIOUS
TREND REPORTS

The farther backward you can look,
the farther forward you can see.
—Winston Churchill

PART I

THE ART OF TREND CURATION

INTRODUCTION

"I AM NOT A SPEED READER, I AM A SPEED UNDERSTANDER."

—ISAAC ASIMOV, Author, Historian and Biochemist

Isaac Asimov was not just a science fiction writer.

In his prolific lifetime, he wrote nearly 500 books on topics ranging from his beloved science fiction series to a two-volume work explaining the collected literature of William Shakespeare. He even wrote a reader's guidebook to the Bible.

Even though he was celebrated for his science fiction work, Asimov never defined himself in one category. When asked which his favorite book was, he often joked, "the last one I've written." He wasn't a scientist or a theologian or a literary critic. He was simply a writer with an incredible curiosity for ideas.

Unlike other experts, he knew that the power of his thinking came from his ability to bring disparate bodies of knowledge together and add his own insight. In fact, he used to describe himself as a "speed understander," a skill he clearly relied on to help him maintain a grueling schedule of publishing more than 15 books a year at his peak.

What if each of us could become a "speed understander" like Asimov? I believe we can.

The simple aim of this book is to teach you how to see the things that others miss. I call that "non-obvious" thinking, and learning how to do it can change your business and your career.

The context within which I'll talk about this type of thinking is business trends. For better or worse, most of us are fascinated by trends and those who predict them. We see these annual predictions as a glimpse into the future and they capture our imagination.

There's only one problem—most of them are based on guesswork or lazy thinking. They are *obvious* instead of *non-obvious*.

This book was inspired by the landslide of obvious ideas we see published today.

In a world where anyone is one button away from being a self-declared expert, learning to think differently is more important than ever. I believe that observing and curating ideas can lead to a unique understanding of why people choose to buy, sell or believe anything.

This book aims to teach you the skills to avoid the obvious and predict trends for yourself.

A great trend is a unique curated observation about the accelerating present.

Great trends are never predictions about the world 20 years from now. Those are most often guesses or wishful thinking. How many trend forecasters do you think predicted the rise of something like Twitter back in 1997? Exactly zero.

Yet this doesn't mean trends are useless. The most powerful trends offer predictions for the *short-term future* based on observing the present. And knowing the short-term future is more valuable than you may think.

Why Does Trend Curation Matter?

Most of our life decisions happen in the short term, though we may describe them differently. You choose to start a business in the short term. You choose whom to marry in the short term. You change careers from one role to the next, all in the short term.

Long-term decisions start in the short term, so understanding how the world is changing in real time is far more valuable immediately than trying to guess what will happen in the world 20 years from now.

When I speak on stage, I often describe myself first as a "trend curator." The reason I use that term is because it describes my passion for collecting ideas and taking the time to see the patterns in them to describe the world in new and interesting ways.

For the past four years, I have published a curated look at the 15 biggest trends that will shape the business world in the year to come. Each year it is called the *Non-Obvious Trend Report* and each edition is based on a year of research, conversation, thinking and writing.

Across that time, I have advised some of the largest brands in the world on business strategy, taught marketing courses at Georgetown University and spoken at events in 27 countries around the world.

All of this gives me the valuable chance to work in dozens of different industries and study media, culture, marketing, technology, design and economics with an unfiltered eye. Each year, I also read or review dozens of books, and buy magazines on everything from cloud computing to Amish farming methods.

I collect these ideas the way frequent fliers collect miles—as momentary rewards to use for later redemption.

Why I Wrote This Book

Unlike many other trend forecasters, simply sharing my annual report is not enough. If I really believe in the value of curating trends, and that anyone can learn to do it, then it was important for me to share my process for how to do it.

So this book is divided into three simple sections.

Part I is dedicated to my methods of trend curation, which I have previously only shared in depth through private workshops or with my students in class. You will learn the greatest myths of trend prediction, five essential habits of trend curators and my own step-by-step approach to curating trends, which I call the Haystack Method.

Part II is the 2015 edition of the *Non-Obvious Trend Report*, featuring 15 new ideas that will shape business in the year to come. Each trend features supporting stories and research, as well as ideas for how to apply the trend to your own business or career.

Part III is filled with tips on making trends actionable, including step-by-step guides to four different types of workshops I use often. In this part, I also discuss the importance of anti-trends (Chapter 15) and how to use "intersection thinking" to see the patterns between industries and stories.

As a bonus, I have also included an extensive collection of appendices which include summaries from every one of my curated trends from four previous editions of the report (more than 60 total), along with candid, honest "longevity ratings" of how accurate those trends still are in 2015.

You can choose to read this book in the order it was published or you can skip back and forth between trends and techniques. Whether you choose to focus on my predictions for 2015 and how to apply them, or learning the techniques of trend curation and non-obvious thinking for yourself, this book is written to be read in short bursts.

Like Asimov, you don't need to be a speed *reader*.

Being a speed *understander*, however, is a worthy aspiration. It is my hope that this book will help you get there.

THE NORWEGIAN BILLIONAIRE:
Why Most Trend Predictions Are Spectacularly Useless

In 1996 Christian Ringnes was a billionaire with the ultimate first-world problem.

One of the richest men in Norway, Ringnes is well known as a flamboyant businessman and art collector whose family started the country's largest brewery more than a hundred years ago. In his hometown of Oslo, Ringnes owns restaurants and museums, and recently donated more than $70 million for the creation of a large sculpture and cultural park, which opened in 2013.

In his heart, Ringnes is a collector. Over decades he has built one of the largest private collections of art in the world. Yet his real legacy may come from something far more unique: his lifelong obsession with collecting mini liquor bottles.

This fixation on mini liquor bottles began for Ringnes at the age of seven when he received an unusual gift from his father: a half-empty miniature liquor bottle. It was this afterthought of a gift that led him on a path towards amassing what is recognized today as the largest independent mini-bottle collection in the world with over 52,000 miniature liquor bottles.

Unfortunately, his decades-long obsession eventually ran into an insurmountable opponent—his wife, Denise.

As the now legendary story goes, Denise wasn't too happy with the disorganization of having all these bottles around the house. After years of frustration, she offered him an ultimatum: either find something to do with all those bottles or start selling them.

Like any avid collector, Ringnes couldn't bear the thought of selling them, so he created a perfectly obvious solution based on his wealth and personality.

He commissioned a museum.

"To Collect Is Human"

Today the Mini Bottle Gallery in downtown Oslo is one of the world's top quirky museum destinations, routinely featured in irreverent travel guides and global lists of must-see Scandinavian tourist attractions. Beyond providing a place for Ringnes to put all of his mini bottles, the gallery is also a popular event venue with an in-house restaurant.

It was this event space and restaurant that offered me my first personal introduction to Ringnes and his story. I was in Oslo for an event and the conference team had organized a tour and dinner at the Mini Bottle Gallery.

It lived up to its quirky reputation.

The entrance to the museum was a bottle shaped hallway leading into an open lobby with a champagne waterfall. As you moved from room to room, each featured its own composed soundtrack, customized lighting and unique smells.

I have 52,500 different miniature bottles in a museum in Oslo. They're completely useless. But men, we like collecting. We like having things. That's human. Once you get fascinated by something, you want it and then you start collecting.

—Christian Ringnes
(From interview in Arterritory.com magazine)

Only steps into the tour, it was clear the gallery was more than just stacks of bottles lined along the walls of a display case in random fashion. Like all great museum experiences, the rooms of the Mini Bottle Gallery had been carefully *curated*.

The mini bottles were grouped into intriguing themes ranging from a brothel themed Room of Sin with mini-bottles from the Dutch Red Light District, to a Horror Room featuring liquor bottles with trapped objects floating inside like mice and worms.

There was a Jungle Room, a Room of Famous Persons, and rooms themed around sports, fruits, birds, circus performers and the occult. And of course, an entire room featured the iconic porcelain series of the Delft Blue KLM houses, a series of tiny Dutch rowhouse-shaped liquor bottles given away to passengers by KLM Airlines for more than five decades.

Across all these rooms, the gallery typically has more than 12,000 bottles on display at any one time. The rest are stored in a bottle vault below the museum and available for display when needed.

Adding Meaning to Noise

If you consider the amount of media any of us is exposed to on an average day, the quest to find meaning amongst the noise is a familiar challenge. Navigating information overload requires a single important skill: curation.

Curation is the ultimate method of transforming noise into meaning.

The Mini Bottle Gallery only displays about 20% of Ringnes' full collection at any time, and carefully keeps the rest in storage. This thoughtful curation makes the experience of seeing them valuable.

Without curation, the meaning would be lost and the experience, meaningless.

An Accidental Trend Curator

It was only on my flight home from Oslo that I realized how important curation had become for my own work.

Just a few months earlier I had published the first edition of my *Non-Obvious Trend Report*, inspired by an idea to publish a blog post from the many ideas I had collected over the past year but never written about.

What I was already doing without realizing it was collecting intriguing ideas and saving them in perhaps the most disorganized way possible—by writing them down, printing them out or ripping them out of magazines and keeping them in a folder on my desk.

In producing that first report, my ambition became to describe patterns in the stories I had collected that went beyond the typical obvious observations I was always reading online. My goal was to find and develop insights that others either hadn't yet noticed or that were not getting the attention they warranted.

To get a different output, sometimes you need a different input.

On that flight home from Norway, I realized that my accidental method for getting different input—collecting ideas for a year and waiting months before analyzing them—could actually be the very thing that would set my insights apart and make them truly non-obvious.

The *Non-Obvious Trend Report* was born from my desire to curate trends on a timeline and scale that others weren't.

Science's Dirty Little Secret

Now, if you happen to be an analytical person, this explanation will hardly seem rigorous enough to be believable. How can collecting ideas and waiting possibly be a recipe for developing genuine insights? What about proper research? What about trend panels and using a global army of spotters? What about the *science*?

Well, it turns out science isn't always done the way we think it is—and that may be a good thing.

In early 2013, a PhD candidate named Beckie Port gathered and published 75 examples of scientists using the hilariously viral hashtag #overlyhonestmethods to share some brutally honest truths about the realities of scientific research.

Among the compilation of tweets Port shared online were these entertaining sound bites:

- "Samples were prepared by our collaborators at MIT. We assumed no contamination because, well... they're MIT #overlyhonestmethods" (@paulcoxon)

- "Our representative device is representative of the ones which didn't immediately explode. #overlyhonestmethods" (@ajdecon)
- "Barbados was selected as a case study because the authors had a naive hope that it might justify some fieldwork there. #overlyhonestmethods" (@mlkubik)
- "We used jargon instead of plain English to prove that a decade of grad school and postdoc made us smart. #overly-honestmethods" (@eperlste)

When you think about the discipline that goes into scientific research and the many years of study that lead to a PhD, it is easy to see research as a task only performed by robot-like perfectionists. The truth of scientific research, just like the truth behind many equally complex areas of study, is that the people behind them are far more human than we tend to admit.

Trends, like science, are not always perfectly observed phenomena that fit neatly into a spreadsheet to be described. This doesn't mean they don't have immense value.

Great science always involves great observation. Scientists learn to observe the results of their experiments and then work to describe them with hypothesis and proof as best they can. Sometimes they do it and sometimes they don't.

For all the similarities between trends and science, this is only half the story. Discovering real trends takes a willingness to combine curiosity with observation and add insight to create valuable ideas that you can then test to ensure they work.

This is vastly different from the method we often mistakenly believe is behind most work with trends, "trend spotting." This phrase is a symbol of some of the many myths we tend to believe about those who predict or describe trends.

Let's explore the five most common of these myths.

The 5 Myths of Trend Spotting

As a writer and speaker, I spend a lot of time seeking stories. When it comes to trends and predicting the future, the people who do this are often called "trend spotters."

Despite what you may have heard, there is no such thing as a trend spotter.

Unfortunately, this trend-spotter bias has created an unreliable picture of the type of person who can predict the future. Consider this lazy definition from WiseGeek.com for what it takes to become a trend spotter:

To become a trend spotter, someone usually receives extensive education and training in the industry he or she is interested in working for. After receiving a thorough grounding in the mechanics and history of the industry, the trend spotter could start working in company departments which predicted trends, slowly working to the rank of an official trend spotter.

The assumption that you need to be working in "company departments which predicted trends" is just plain idiotic.

I believe that anyone can learn the right habits to train themselves on becoming better at curating trends and predicting the future for themselves.

The rest of this first part of the book is dedicated to teaching you to how to curate and uncover trends for yourself, but before we start, it is important to tackle some of the biggest myths surrounding trends so you know what to avoid reading (or trusting!) in case you happen to encounter it in the future.

MYTH #1: TRENDS ARE SPOTTED.

The idea of trend spotting suggests that there are trends simply sitting out there in plain sight ready to be observed and cataloged like avian species for bird watchers. The reality of trends is far different. Trend spotters typically find individual examples or stories. Calling the multitude of things they spot the same thing as trends is like calling eggs, flour and sugar sitting on a shelf the same thing as a cake. You can "spot" ingredients, but trends must be curated from these ingredients in order to have meaning.

MYTH #2: TRENDS ARE PREDICTED BY INDUSTRY GURUS/EXPERTS.

It is tempting to see expertise as a prerequisite to being good at curating trends, but there is also a predictable drawback: blind spots. Quite simply, the more you know about a particular topic, the more difficult it becomes to think outside your expertise and broaden your view. There is no single expertise required to curate trends, but those with a greater curiosity about the world beyond any industry will more easily avoid any danger of industry-based tunnel vision.

MYTH #3: TRENDS ARE BASED ON HARD DATA.

When it comes to any type of research, some people rely on numbers inserted into a spreadsheet as proof, and they conveniently forget that there are two methods to gathering research: the quantitative method *and* the qualitative method. Qualitative research involves using observation and experience to gather mainly verbal data instead of results from experiments. If you are uncovering the perfect pH balance for shampoo, you definitely want to use quantitative research. For curating trends, you need a mixture of both and the ability to remember that hard data can often be less important than really good observation.

MYTH #4: TRENDS ONLY REFLECT CURRENT POPULARITY.

The line between trends and fads can be tricky. Although some trends seem to spotlight a currently popular story, good ones need to describe something that happens over a span of time. Fads, in comparison, describe an idea that is popular in the short term. Great trends do reflect a moment in time, but they also need to describe something that is broader than a fleeting moment.

MYTH #5: TRENDS ARE HOPELESSLY BROAD PREDICTIONS.

Perhaps no other myth about trends is as fueled by reality as this one. The fact is, we encounter hopelessly broad trend predictions in the media all the time. The problem comes in treating those as indications that trends *should* be broad and all encompassing. Good trends tend to be the exact opposite. They define something that is concrete and distinct. Something that doesn't apply to everyone, but rather offers a point of view that you can easily grasp and describe in a unique way.

Now that I have shared five of the most common myths about trend predictions, we need to spend a brief moment talking about a sad but true fact about many trend predictions you might end up reading.

In our one-button world of publishing opinions online, many of trend predictions you might read are little more than self-indulgent guesswork or lazy thinking. At this point, you could be forgiven for wondering why I am so negative on so many other trend predictions out there. Why exactly do I dismiss them as useless?

In order to illustrate, let me tell you a little story.

Why (Most) Trend Predictions Are Useless

A few weeks ago I picked up the final 2014 edition of *Entrepreneur* magazine which promised to illuminate trends to watch in 2015. Earlier that same week, a special double issue of *BusinessWeek* magazine arrived in the mail making a similar promise.

It was December and the trend season was in full swing.

Just like New Year's resolutions to lose weight, trend forecasting is what everyone starts talking about at the end of the year. Unfortunately, the side effect of this annual media ritual is an abundance of lazy predictions and vague declarations.

For entertainment over the years, I have started to collect them as standing memorials to the volume of pitiful predictions each of us have become used to confronting at the end of every year.

To illustrate my point, here are a few of the worst offending most obvious "trends" shared near the end of 2014. For the sake of kindness, I removed reference to which particular publication or writer a trend came from before listing them below:

- "It's all about the content."
- "Integration"
- "The Year Of Mobile has arrived. Really."
- "Public Relations will continue to be the place to be."

- ·"Google Plus"
- "3D Printing"
- "Change will be led by wearable technology and augmented reality."

Integration? Really?

Not to ruin the suspense, but I don't believe any of these are actually trends. Some are just random buzzwords or the names of platforms. Others are hopelessly broad, useless and, yes, obvious.

None is a unique idea describing the accelerating present.

Meanwhile, all of us as media consumers watch all of it unfold with varying levels of skepticism. Trend predictions have a believability problem, but I think it can be solved. In order to do that, a perfect place to start is by understanding the four reasons why most trend predictions fail so spectacularly.

REASON 1: NO OBJECTIVITY

If you sell hammers, declaring 2015 the "Year of Hammers" is clearly self-serving. Of course, most bias isn't this easy to spot and objectivity is notoriously difficult for any of us. Our biases are based on our expertise and the world we know. This is particularly true in business where we sometimes *need* to believe in industry or brand in order to succeed. The problem is, losing objectivity usually leads to wishful thinking. Just because we want something to be a trend doesn't make it one.

> *EXAMPLE: Near the end of 2014, I received what seemed like dozens of emails about white papers and blog posts each forecasting that wearable technology or the "Internet of things" would be the hottest trend of the coming year. Unsurprisingly, the vast majority of them had some type of product or strategy to cash in on this hot trend— and were mostly dismissed by the media they were aiming to reach.*

REASON 2: NO CREATIVITY

Trends need to do more than repeat common knowledge. For example, saying that "more people will buy tablets in 2015" is obvious—and useless because it lacks creativity. The biggest reason that most trend predictions share these types of hopelessly obvious ideas is because it is easier to do so. Lazy thinking is always easier than creative and informed thinking. Great trends are never obvious declarations of fact that most people already know. They share new ideas in insightful ways while also describing the accelerating present.

EXAMPLE: The phrase "digital natives" was first coined nearly 15 years ago to describe a generation who would grow up never having known a world before the Internet. Despite its long history and relative ubiquity, several trend articles I reviewed at the end of 2014 shared the "emergence" of this group as if it were a brand new insight. That's just plain lazy.

REASON 3: NO PROOF

Sharing a trend without specific examples is like declaring yourself a musician by simply buying a guitar and learning to play one song. Unfortunately, many trend predictions coast on the power of a single story or example. Great examples and stories are powerful parts of illustrating why a trend matters. They are necessary elements of proving a trend. Only finding one (or none) and declaring something a trend without them is usually a sign that a so-called trend is based on little more than guesswork.

EXAMPLE: When publishing website Medium.com first became publicly available and increasing numbers of journalists and writers began using it to freely share extremely high-quality stories and articles, several early trend reports in 2014 predicted the rise of a sort of anti-Twitter trend where people would begin flocking to longer-form content. Unfortunately, one popular website isn't enough to describe a trend, and most of these forecasts were predictable failures.

REASON 4: NO APPLICATION

Perhaps the most common place where many trend predictions fall short is in the discussion of how to apply them. It is not enough to think about trends in the context of describing them. Aside from that being one of the myths behind finding trends, it also provides little value because it isn't clear what someone might do differently as a result of understanding a particular trend. The best trend predictions go further than just describing something that is happening. They also share insights on what it means and what you can do to use the trend in your own situation. In other words, their trends are actionable.

EXAMPLE: In a beautiful piece of ironic content, a collaboration of top PR agencies published a sponsored editorial in Advertising Age *magazine last year aimed at sharing predictions for the upcoming year to underscore the value of PR for big clients. Unfortunately, most of the top ten predictions featured plentiful buzzword babble, like "Big data is important, but big insights are critical" and was dramatically short on any real insights on how to apply the thinking or what to do about it. Not the PR industry's best work.*

How to Think Different about Trends

Now that you've reached the end of this chapter, you are probably wondering what actually makes a great trend when there are so many myths and reasons for failure.

What actually makes a trend, and what makes it non-obvious?

A non-obvious trend is an idea that describes the accelerating present in a new, unique way.

The next two chapters will share a step-by-step approach to help you think differently about trends and escape the trap of lazy thinking and flawed insights. The biggest challenge is learning to abandon the obvious ideas and push yourself to work harder.

When you do, I guarantee that not only will your ideas improve, but your outlook on your business and your career will as well.

So, let's get started.

THE CURATOR'S MINDSET:
Learning the 5 Essential Habits of Trend Curators

In 2006, renowned Stanford psychology professor Carol Dweck wrote a book about an idea so simple it hardly seemed worth mentioning—much less devoting an entire book to exploring.

Across decades of research into motivation, achievement and success, Dweck had come upon a beautifully elegant idea to describe why some people succeeded while others failed: it all came down to *mindsets*.

After conducting experiments with grade school students, interviewing professional athletes and studying business leaders, Dweck proposed that most people had one of two types of mindsets: a fixed mindset or a growth mindset.

People with *fixed mindsets*, argued Dweck, believe that their skills and abilities are set. They see themselves as either being either good at something or not good at something, and therefore tend to focus their efforts on tasks and in careers where they feel they have a natural ability.

People with *growth mindsets* believe that success and achievement are the result of hard work and determination. They see their own (and others') true potential as something to be defined through effort. As a result, they thrive on challenges and often have a passion for learning.

It likely won't surprise you to learn that I believe in the power of the growth mindset and aspire to always maintain one for myself. When it comes to learning to predict the future, though, it is important to adopt that same mindset for yourself.

The beautiful thing about mindsets is that we all have the ability to change ours—we just need to make the choice to do it.

Seeing trends, like playing the guitar or being more observant, are skills within your grasp to learn and practice. Does this mean you can transform yourself into a professional flamenco guitarist or a full-time trend forecaster with enough practice? Not necessarily. Aptitude and natural talent do play an important part in succeeding at anything on a professional level.

Still, my work with hundreds of executives and students at all levels of their careers has proved to me that the skills required for trend curation can be learned and practiced. When you learn them, they can inform your own view of the world and power your own future success.

> *As soon as children become able to evaluate themselves, some of them become afraid of challenges. They become afraid of not being smart. I have studied thousands of people ... and it's breathtaking how many reject an opportunity to learn.*
>
> —Carol Dweck (from *Mindset*)

Beyond adopting the growth mindset and having a willingness to learn, there are five core habits that will help you develop your trend-curation abilities. Let's explore them by starting with a story of the most famous art collector most people have never heard of—until he passed away.

The Unlikely Curator

By 2012, at the ripe old age of 89 years, a retired postal worker had quietly amassed one of the greatest collections of modern art in the world.

Herbert Vogel and his wife, Dorothy, were already legends in the world of art when Herbert passed away. News stories the day after his death told the story of five large moving vans showing up at the Vogel's rent-controlled, one-bedroom New York apartment to pick up more than 5000 pieces of art. This Vogel Collection, built over decades, would have a permanent home as part of the archives and collection at the National Gallery of Art.

The Vogels always said the only things they did were buy and collect art they loved.

This passion often led them to find new young artists to support before the rest of the world discovered them. The Vogels ultimately became more than collectors. They were tastemakers and their "fabled collection," as one critic later described it, which included art from hundreds of artists including pop artist Roy Lichtenstein and post-minimalist Richard Tuttle, was the envy of museums around the world.

The same qualities that drive art patrons like the Vogels to follow their instincts and collect beautiful things are the ones that make great curators of any kind.

The Rise Of "Curationism"

Museum curators organize collections into themes that tell stories. Whether they're quirky like those told in the Mini Bottle Gallery, or an expansive exhibit at the Metropolitan Museum of Art, the goal of curation is always taking individual items and examples and weaving them together into a narrative.

Curators add meaning to isolated beautiful things.

I am inspired by curators—and I am clearly not alone. The business world has turned toward the longtime practice of curation with such growing frequency that even the world of artists and art critics has begun to notice.

In 2014, art critic and writer David Balzer published a book with the brilliant title *Curationism* (a play on creationism) to explore how "curating took over the art world and everything else." His book explores the evolution of the curator as the "imparter of value."

The one caution he shares in his book is that this rise in curationism can sometimes inspire a "constant cycle of grasping and display" where we never take the time to understand what all the pieces mean. In business *or* art, curation is only valuable if you follow the act of collecting information with enough moments of "quiet contemplation" to truly understand what you are seeing and collecting.

This combination of collection and contemplation is central to being able to effectively curate ideas and learn to predict the future. To do it, there are five specific habits that I believe can help you find the right amount of time for this sort of thinking in a world that seldom seems to offer you the time for such a luxury.

Let's explore these five habits further.

The 5 Habits Of Trend Curators

Curators come from all types of backgrounds.

Some focus on art and design while others may look at history or anthropology. Some have professional training and degrees and others are driven by passion like Herbert and Dorothy Vogel. No matter their background, every one of them exhibits the same types of habits that help them to become masters at adding meaning to collected items.

Curation doesn't require you to be an expert or a researcher or an academic. Learning these five habits will help you put the power of curation to work to help you discover better ideas and use them to develop smarter observations about the rapidly accelerating present.

THE 5 HABITS OF TREND CURATORS

1. **BEING CURIOUS** – always wanting to know why and always seeking to learn more about the world and improve your knowledge by investigating and asking questions.

2. **BEING OBSERVANT** – learning to see the small details in stories and activities that others may ignore or fail to recognize as significant.

3. **BEING FICKLE** – moving from one idea to the next without becoming fixated, developing deep biases or overanalyzing each idea in the moment.

4. **BEING THOUGHTFUL** – taking enough time to develop a meaningful point of view and patiently considering alternative viewpoints before finalizing an idea.

5. **BEING ELEGANT** – seeking beautiful ways to describe ideas that bring together disparate concepts in a simple and understandable way.

For the past five years I have been sharing and teaching these habits through workshops and classes to business professionals, entrepreneurs and university students. I have learned one simple thing from that experience: we all have the aptitude to learn these skills. The challenge always comes from teaching yourself to apply them.

To help, let's take a deeper look at each skill and some actionable ways to learn how to use them.

How to Be Curious

Bjarni Herjulfsson could have been one of the most famous explorers of his time.

Instead, his life has become a cautionary tale about the perils of lacking curiosity. In the year 986, he set off on a voyage from Norway with a crew to find Greenland. Blown off course by a storm, his ship became the first European vessel in recorded history to see North America.

Despite his crew pleading to stop and explore, Herjulfsson refused and guided his ship back on course to eventually find Greenland. Years later, he told this tale to a friend of his named Leif Eriksson who became inspired, purchased Herjulfsson's ship and took the journey for himself.

As many of us learned in grade school, Erikson is now widely remembered as the first European to land in North America—nearly 500 years before Christopher Columbus. Herjulfsson's story illustrates one of the most compelling facts about curiosity (or a lack of it): curiosity is a prerequisite to discovery.

Being more curious means asking questions about why things work the way they do and embracing unfamiliar situations or topics with a sense of wonder.

We as people are naturally curious. The challenge is to continually find ways to allow yourself to explore your curiosity without it feeling like an ongoing distraction.

When noted chef and food pioneer Ferran Adrià was once asked what he likes to have for breakfast, his reply was simple: "I like to eat a different fruit every day of the month."

Imagine if you were able to do that with ideas.

Part of being curious is wanting to consume different things all the time to earn greater knowledge of the world, even if that knowledge doesn't seem immediately useful. Here are some ways to do it:

REAL LIFE ADVICE (3 WAYS TO BE MORE CURIOUS TODAY)

✓ **Consume "Brainful Media"** – Sadly we are surrounded with what I like to call "brainless media," including reality shows featuring unlikeable people doing unlikeable things (sometimes on islands, sometimes in our backyards). While sometimes entertaining, brainless media also encourages vegetation instead of curiosity. Curiosity is far better developed by consuming "brainful media," such as a short documentary film or inspirational 17-minute talk from TED.com.

✓ **Empathize with Magazines** – Curiosity comes from seeing the world through someone else's eyes, even if it's uncomfortable. I often use niche magazines to learn about unfamiliar things. Simply walking into the magazine section of a bookstore or visiting www.magazines.com offers plenty of options. For example, *The Progressive Farmer*, *Model Railroader* and *House Beautiful* are three vastly different magazines. Flipping through the stories, advertisements and imagery in each will do more to take you outside of your own world than almost any other quick and easy activity.

✓ **Ask Bigger Questions** – Several months ago, I was invited to deliver a talk at an event for the paint industry. It is an industry I know very little about and so it would have been easy to show up, deliver my talk and then leave. Instead, I stayed and walked around the exhibit hall asking questions. In less than 30 minutes I learned about how paint is mixed and what additives are typically used. I heard about the industry debate between all-plastic cans versus steel and the rise of computerized color matching systems. The only reason I learned about any of these things was because I chose to stay and ask more questions instead of taking the easy path and leaving early.

WHAT TO READ

✓ **Historical Fiction** – Every great piece of historical fiction was inspired by a writer who found a story in history that was worth retelling and sharing with the world. This curiosity makes books like Erik Larsen's *The Devil In The White City* (about murder at the 1893 Chicago World's Fair) or Simon Winchester's *The Professor And the Madman* (about the creation of the *Oxford English Dictionary*) wonderful tools to get you thinking about the world in new and unexpected ways.

✓ **Curated Compilations** – There are many books that bring together real life stories or essays to help you think about new and interesting topics. A collection of shorter topics and stories is sometimes far easier to use for engaging your curiosity than a longer book. For example, the *This Will Make You Smarter* series edited by John Brockman or any book by You Are Not So Smart founder and psychology nerd David McRaney are perfect, bite-sized ways to inspire your curiosity without requiring a huge time investment.

How to Be Observant

Last year I was invited to a formal dinner at an event in New York. The venue was a beautiful restaurant and after our meal the waiter came around to take our dessert orders from one of two set menu options. Less than 10 minutes later, a team of six people *not* including our waiter came and delivered all the desserts to our large table of 30 people, getting each order perfectly right without saying a word to anyone.

As they delivered the desserts, I started to wonder how had that one waiter who took our orders managed to relay all those choices perfectly to a team of six within 10 minutes?

By observing, I quickly figured out the simple trick our head waiter had used. If you had picked dessert option one, he placed a dessert spoon *above* your plate. And if you picked option two, he placed the spoon to the *right* of your plate.

So when that team of food runners came to the table, all they needed was the "code" to decipher the spoon positioning and they would be able to deliver the desserts perfectly. That little story of food delivery is a perfect example of why observation matters.

Being more observant means training yourself to see the details that most others often miss.

Perhaps you already knew that little spoon trick, but imagine you didn't. Simply observing it could teach you something fascinating about the little processes that we rarely pay attention to that keep the world moving along. Now imagine that moment multiplied by a hundred or a thousand.

Learning to be more observant isn't about seeing the big things. Instead, it is about training yourself to pay more attention to the little things.

By simply choosing to observe, what can you see about a situation that no one else notices?

What can that teach you about people, processes and companies that you didn't know before?

This is the power of making observation a habit, so let's explore three ways to help you do it.

REAL LIFE ADVICE
(3 WAYS TO BE MORE OBSERVANT TODAY)

✓ **Explain the World to Children** – If you are lucky enough to have children in your life, one of the best ways to train yourself to use observation more frequently is to get better about explaining the world around you to children. When my kids asked me recently why construction vehicles and traffic signs are orange but cars aren't, it forced me to think about things I would otherwise have easily ignored, even if I didn't have the perfect answer to the question.

✓ **Watch Processes in Action** – Every situation is filled with processes, from how school buses drop off children at their stops to how coffee shops take and make orders every morning. When you look at these interactions, you'll notice that nothing is by accident. Pay attention and ask yourself what does a typical interaction look like? How does it differ when it involves a "regular" versus a "newbie"? Seeing these patterns in regular everyday life can help you train yourself to use this observational skill in other situations as well.

✓ **Don't Be Observationally Lazy** – It is easy to go through the mundane moments of life glued to your smartphone. Aside from being really good at capturing our attention (see Chapter 15 on *Engineered Addiction*), they also keep us from seeing the world around us. Rather than switching to auto-pilot to navigate daily tasks like commuting or buying groceries, train yourself to put your phone down and choose to be observant instead.

WHAT TO READ

✓ *What Every Body Is Saying* **by Joe Navarro** – If you need to learn the art of interpreting body language or detecting lies, a former FBI agent like Joe Navarro is probably the ideal teacher. In this best selling book from 2008, Navarro shares some of his best lessons on how to spot tells in body language and use them to interpret human behavior. His work on situational awareness and teaching people *how* to be more observant to assess people and situations for danger and comfort is a brilliant book that should be on your reading list no matter what you do. It also happens to be a perfect supporting book to teach you how to be more observant in general.

How to Be Fickle

Being fickle may seem like a bad thing, but that isn't always true.

When we hear the word, we tend to think of all the negative situations where we act in inconstantly or abandon people or ideas too quickly, but there is an upside to learning how to be purposefully fickle.

Being fickle means capturing ideas without needing to fully understand or analyze them in that same moment.

On the surface, this may seem counterintuitive. After all, when you find a great idea why wouldn't you take the time to analyze it and develop a point of view? There are certainly many situations when you will want to do that, and chances are you do it already.

But you probably *never* do the opposite. A part of becoming an idea curator is saving ideas for later digestion. This doesn't always mean you don't think about them when you find them, but you don't always *need* to.

For example, here are three interesting stories which I recently saw and saved:

- Coca-Cola decided to disconnect voicemail for all employees at its corporate headquarters in Atlanta.
- Richard Branson allows Virgin staff to take as much holiday as they want.
- A Trader Joe's employee gave a gift of flowers to a flustered mom of adopted kids who was leaving the store after an embarrassing toddler meltdown because the employee herself had been adopted and she just wanted to say thanks.

When I saved each of the stories above, I didn't make the broader connection to tie them together. Only when I reviewed them at the end of the year while researching trends did I realize that each of these stories says something unique about the state of employee relationships with their employers and empowerment.

There was a theme, but it was only by setting those stories aside and choosing to analyze them later that I had enough perspective to see that connection. Being fickle isn't about avoiding thought—it is about freeing yourself from the time constraints you might feel around collecting ideas by making it easier to save an idea without necessarily analyzing it deeply in the moment.

To help you learn to do the same thing, here are some tips.

REAL LIFE ADVICE (3 WAYS TO BE MORE FICKLE TODAY)

✓ **Save Ideas Offline** – Thanks to wonderful productivity apps like Evernote and plenty of browser plugins, there are many ways to save information online, but they can sometimes be lost in collections you never return to and the connections between them are hard to visualize. Instead, I routinely print articles, rip stories out of magazines and save them into a *single* trend folder which sits on my desk. Saving ideas offline allows me to spread them out later to analyze more easily, but it also helps me avoid overanalyzing them in that moment when I find them.

✓ **Use a Timer** – If given the chance, most of us will naturally take the time to analyze something that we see or find in a moment. Being fickle is partially about intentionally delaying that process and using a timer can help. The other benefit of literally using a timer when you are consuming some type of new media is that it forces you to evaluate things more quickly and then leave them behind as you move to something else.

✓ **Take Notes with Sharpies** – Many of the articles and stories I find throughout the year are marked with just a few words about the theme of the article and story. I use the Sharpie because the thicker lettering stands out and encourages me subtly to write less because it takes up much more space. This same trick can help you to make only the most useful observations in the moment and save any other ones for later.

WHAT TO READ

✓ *The Laws Of Simplicity* by John Maeda – Maeda is a master of design and technology and his advice has guided many companies and entrepreneurs toward building more amazing products. In this exactly 100-page book, he shares some essential advice for learning to see the world like a designer and reduce the noise to see and think more clearly. "More appears like less by simply moving it far, far away," he writes when talking about the power of software as a service or the value of Google. I believe the same principle applies to information and ideas; sometimes you just need distance and time in order to fully appreciate them.

How to Be Thoughtful

In 2014 after 10 years of writing my personal blog, I decided to stop allowing comments. This seemed counter to the fundamental principle of blogging, which is to create a dialogue (as many of my readers emailed to tell me). Was it because I thought I was too important to answer comments, or was there something else at work?

The reason I stopped was simple. I had noticed a steady decline in the quality of comments over the 10 years that I had been blogging. What was once a robust discussion that involved thoughtfully worded responses had devolved into a combination of thumbs-up style comments and spam.

Thanks to anonymous commenting and the ease of sharing knee-jerk responses, comments had become *thoughtless* instead of *thoughtful*—and many people online were starting to notice.

Unfortunately, the Internet is filled with this type of "conversation."

Being thoughtful means taking the time to reflect on a point of view and share it in a considered way.

Despite this general shift in online commenting, there is one platform that hopes to single-handedly change this landscape. In 2012 LinkedIn launched a pilot program called *LinkedIn Influencers* to feature insights from top business minds like Tom Peters and Bill Gates, who answered compelling questions like what advice they might offer to their 20-year-old selves.

These posts inspired amazingly detailed and well-thought-out comments from LinkedIn users. Every comment was linked to a professional profile, and the stature of the contributors led to better comments. After all, who would post an ill-informed stupid comment if they thought Bill Gates might actually read it?

Online commenting might seem like a relatively frivolous way to illustrate the value of being thoughtful, but it is just a symbol of how important taking the time to consider an argument has become.

To help you be more thoughtful as you think about curating trends and understanding the media that you save and consume every day, here are some tips:

REAL LIFE ADVICE
(3 WAYS TO BE MORE THOUGHTFUL TODAY)

✓ **Wait a Moment** – The beauty and challenge of the Internet is that it occurs in real time. We have an idea, and we can share it immediately. It's easy to think that if you can't be the first person to comment on something, that your thoughts are too late. That is rarely true. Real time should not mean sharing a comment from the top of your head within seconds. Instead, you need to redefine it so your comment is still relevant beyond the particular moment you write it. This means you might choose to take 15 minutes (or longer!) to think about *how* you want to share it.

✓ **Write and then Rewrite** – Anyone who has ever had to write consistently will tell you that the ultimate way to get better at writing is to just force yourself to do it even if whatever comes out isn't very usable. When it comes to being thoughtful with writing, even the most talented writers take the time to rewrite instead of simply sharing the first thing that they write down.

✓ **Embrace the Pauses** – One of the things speakers try to learn as soon as they spend any time standing in front of an audience is how to become comfortable with silence. It's not an easy thing to do. Yet when you can use pauses effectively, you can emphasize the things you really want people to hear or remember. This same principle works whether you are on stage or just engaged in a conversation. The trick is to use those pauses as times to find the right words so you *can* be more thoughtful when you eventually do share your point of view.

WHAT TO READ

✓ *Brain Pickings* by **Maria Popova** - Popova describes herself as an "interestingness hunter-gatherer" and she writes Brain Pickings, one of the most popular independently run blogs in the world. On the site she publishes articles combining lessons from literature, art and history on wide ranging topics like creative leadership and the gift of friendship. Every year she pores thousands of hours into publishing thoughtful pieces and her readers reward her by donating to support the continued ad-free operation of the site. The way she presents her thoughts is a perfect intellectual example of how to publish something thoughtful week after week.

How to Be Elegant

Jeff Karp is a scientist inspired by elegance ... and jellyfish.

As an associate professor at Harvard Medical School, Karp's research focuses on using bio-inspiration—inspiration from nature—to develop new solutions for all types of medical challenges. His self-named Karp Lab has developed innovations such as a device inspired by jellyfish tentacles to capture circulating tumor cells in cancer patients, and better surgical staples inspired by porcupine quills.

Nature is filled with elegant solutions, from the way that forest fires spread the seeds of certain plants to the way termites build porous structures with natural heating and cooling built in.

Ian Glynn, author of the book *Elegance In Science*, argues that elegant proofs or theories have most or all of the following features: they are simple, ingenious, concise and persuasive; they often have an unexpected quality, and they are very satisfying.

I believe it is this idea of simplicity that is fundamental to developing elegant ideas. As Einstein famously said, "make things as simple as possible, but not simpler."

Being elegant means developing your ability to describe a concept in a beautiful and simple way for easy understanding.

A good example of things described beautifully is in what great poets do. If you are out of school, chances are you don't spend much time with poetry. Great poetry has simplicity, and emotion, and beauty *because* words are taken away. Poets are masters of elegance, obsessive over language, and always understand that sometimes less can mean more.

You don't need to become a poet overnight, but some of these principles can help you get better at creating more elegant descriptions of your ideas.

For example, think back to the last time you encountered something that was poetically written. It may have been something you once read in school, or perhaps a Dr. Seuss book that you read to a child at bedtime.

Dr. Seuss in particular had a beautiful talent for sharing big ideas with a simplicity and elegance:

- "Today you are you, that is truer than true. There is no one alive who is youer than you."
- "A person's a person, no matter how small."
- "Everything stinks till it's finished."

We love to read or see elegant solutions and we delight in their ability to help us get the big picture with ease, but they may not seem quite so simple to develop or write. If you have ever sat down with paper or in front of a computer screen and tried to tell a simple story you know that it can be harder than it seems.

But we all have the power to simplify our ideas and share them in more elegant ways. We just need a better way to do it. Here are a few ideas to help.

REAL LIFE ADVICE
(3 WAYS TO THINK MORE ELEGANTLY TODAY)

✓ **Start with the Obvious** – One of my favorite trends from my *2012 Non-Obvious Trend Report* was something I called "ChangeSourcing" to describe the idea that more and more people were turning to crowdfunding campaigns to inspire more movements for social change. At the time, crowdfunding was one of the hottest topics in the media. The idea of ChangeSourcing took something that people already knew in an unexpected new direction and used a simple and elegant title to do it. As a result, it was one of the most talked-about trends from the report that year.

✓ **Keep It Short** – One thing you will notice if you look back on any of my previous trend reports is that no trend is more than two words. Elegance often goes hand in hand with simplicity and this usually translates into using as few words as possible. When it comes to defining and curating trends, it is perfectly fine to start by describing the trend with as many words as you need. When you get to the point of trying to add more elegance to your description, though, a necessary component will usually be reducing the words you use to name *and* describe it.

✓ **Use Poetic Principles** – There are some basic principles that poets use when writing that can also be helpful for anyone who is curating trends. One of them is to try and use metaphors and imagery instead of obvious ways of sharing something. Another is to rhyme words or use alliteration to add symmetry to an idea. If you flip to the second part of this book, you will see many places where I used these types of principles to develop trends like "Branded Benevolence" or "Unperfection"—which may be my favorite trend name from this year's report because of its slight twist from "imperfection" makes it meaningful yet still unique.

WHAT TO READ

✓ *Einstein's Dreams* **by Alan Lightman** – Lightman was the first professor at MIT to receive a joint appointment in the sciences and the humanities and is a trained physicist and a poet. His book *Einstein's Dreams* has been one of my favorites for years because of how it imagines what Einstein's dreams must have been like and explores them in a beautiful way through short chapters with interesting assumptions about time and space. This is not a book of poetry, but it will not only introduce you to the power of poetic writing but also lead you toward the most elegant description of how time might actually work that you'll ever read.

Why *These* 5 Habits?

Looking back, the fact that I only chose 5 habits to help you learn the art of curating ideas may seem a bit random. What makes these five habits stand out? The fact is, the process of how I came to these five in particular was an interesting exercise of curation in itself.

Over the past year, I read interviews with professional art curators and how they learned their craft. I bought more than a dozen books written by trend forecasters, futurists and innovators. I carefully studied my own behavior, and (as I mentioned earlier in the chapter) I tested the effectiveness of these habits by teaching them to my students in classes and business professionals in workshops.

Ultimately, I selected the five habits presented in this chapter because they were the most helpful, descriptive, easy to learn and effective once you learn to put them into action.

So as a final recap before we get started with a step-by-step approach to curating trends, let's do a quick review of the five habits here:

1. **Being *curious*** means asking questions about why things work the way they do, and embracing unfamiliar situations or topics with a sense of wonder.

2. **Being *observant*** means training yourself to see the details that most others often miss.

3. **Being *fickle*** means capturing ideas without feeling the need to fully understand or analyze them in that moment.

4. **Being *thoughtful*** means taking the time to reflect on a point of view and share it in a considered way.

5. **Being *elegant*** means developing your ability to describe a concept in a beautiful and simple way for easy understanding.

5 HABITS OF TREND CURATORS

THE HAYSTACK METHOD:
How to Curate Trends for Fun and Profit

"THE MOST RELIABLE WAY TO ANTICIPATE THE FUTURE
IS THE UNDERSTAND THE PRESENT."

—JOHN NAISBITT, Futurist and Author of *Megatrends*

In 1982, a single book called *Megatrends* changed the way governments, businesses and people thought about the future.

In the book, author John Naisbitt was one of the first to predict our evolution from an industrial society to an information society, and he did so more than a decade before the Internet. He also predicted the shift from hierarchies to networks and the rise of the global economy.

Despite the book's unapologetic American-style optimism, most of the 10 major shifts described in the book were so far ahead of their time that when it was first released one reviewer glowingly described it as "the next best thing to a crystal ball." With over 14 million copies sold worldwide, it is still the single best-selling book about the future published in the last 40 years.

In the decades since the book came out, Naisbitt has been asked the same question in dozens of interviews with the media: how did he develop his ability to predict the future and could others learn to do it?

For his part, Naisbitt believed deeply in the power of observation to understand the present before trying to predict the future (as the opening quote to this chapter illustrates). In interviews, friends and family often described Naisbitt as having a "boundless curiosity about people, cultures and organizations."

A profile piece in *USA Today* back in 2006 even noted his penchant for scanning "hundreds of newspapers and magazines, from *Scientific American* to *Tricycle*, a Buddhism magazine" as a symbol of his incessant desire to learn.

John Naisbitt was and still is (at the age of 86!) a collector of ideas. His story has inspired me for years to think about the world with a similarly broad lens and to develop the method I use for my own trend work: the Haystack Method.

Inside the Haystack Method

It is tempting to describe the art of finding trends with the cliché of finding a "needle in a haystack." This common visual reference brings to mind the myth of trend spotting that I discounted earlier in this section. Uncovering trends hardly ever involves spotting them sitting neatly inside a so-called stack of hay waiting to be discovered.

The Haystack Method describes a process where you first focus on gathering stories and ideas (the hay) and *then* using them to define a trend (the needle) that gives meaning to them all collectively.

In the method, the work comes from assembling the information and curating it into groupings that make sense. The needle is the insight you apply to this collection of information in order to describe what it means—and to curate information and stories into a definable trend.

Trend curators don't seek needles, they gather the hay and stick a needle into the middle of it.

While that describes the method with metaphors, to truly learn how to do it for yourself, we must go much deeper. To do that for the Haystack Method, let's break it down into its five key components.

THE HAYSTACK METHOD

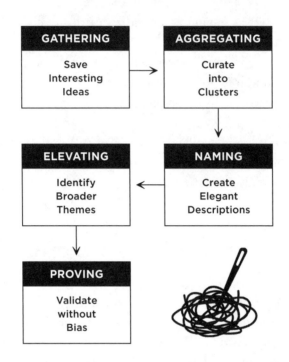

GATHERING	AGGREGATING
Save Interesting Ideas	Curate into Clusters

ELEVATING	NAMING
Identify Broader Themes	Create Elegant Descriptions

PROVING
Validate without Bias

Why I Started Curating Ideas

The Haystick Method was born from frustration.

In 2004, I was part of a team that was starting one of the first social media–focused practices within a large marketing agency. The idea was that we would help big companies figure out how to use social media.

Back then "social media" mainly referred to blogging since it was before Facebook and Twitter. The real aim of our team was to help brands work with influential bloggers. There was only one problem with this well-intentioned plan—none of us knew very much about blogging.

So, we each did the only thing that seemed logical to do: each of us started blogging for ourselves.

In June of that year I started my "Influential Marketing Blog" with an aim to reflect on marketing, public relations and advertising strategy. My first post was on the dull topic of optimal screen size for web designers. Within a few days I ran into my first major problem: I had no idea what to write about next.

How was I going to keep this hastily created blog current with new ideas and stories when I already had a full time day job that didn't officially involve spending time writing a blog?

I started to collect ideas.

At first it was just ideas for blog posts, scratched into a notebook or emailed to myself. Then, I started capturing concepts from the many brainstorms I was involved in on a daily basis. Pretty soon I was saving quotes from books, ripping pages out of magazines and generating plenty of blog posts based on the ideas I had collected.

These first four years of blogging led to my first book deal with McGraw-Hill. Several years later, the desire to write a blog post about trends based on ideas I had collected across the year led me to publish the first edition of my *Non-Obvious Trend Report*.

Collecting ideas led me to create a reputation and audience for myself through blogging, and this process of gathering ideas also happens to be the first step in the Haystack Method.

Step 1—Gathering

Gathering is the simple act of collecting stories and ideas from any interaction you have with people or with content in any form across multiple channels.

Do you read the same sources of media religiously every day? Or do you skim Twitter occasionally and sometimes follow the links to continue reading? Regardless of your media consumption, chances are you encounter plenty of interesting stories or ideas. The real question is, do you save them?

The key to gathering ideas is making a *habit* of saving interesting things.

My method involves always carrying a small Moleskine notebook in my bag and keeping a folder on my desk to save media clippings and printouts. By the time you read these words, that folder on my desk has changed color and already says "2016 Trends" on the outside of it.

In my process, I start the clock every January and complete it each December for my annual *Non-Obvious Trend Report*. Thanks to this deliverable, I have a clear starting and ending point for each new round of ideas that I collect.

You don't need to follow as rigid of a calendar timetable, but it is valuable to set yourself a specific time when you can go back and reflect on what you have gathered to uncover the bigger insights (a point we will explore in subsequent steps).

IDEA SOURCES—Where to Get Ideas

1. Personal conversations at events or meetings (ask lots of questions)

2. Listening to live speakers or TED Talks (write down memorable quotes)

3. Entertainment (TV shows and movies that actually make you think)

4. Books (Nonfiction and fiction)

5. Museums (the more obscure the better!)

6. Magazines and newspapers (as unexpected or outside your realm of knowledge as possible)

7. Travel! (even if it doesn't seem exotic or far away)

As you first read this list of sources, they might seem unsurprising. It is rarely the *sources* of information themselves that will lead you toward a perfectly packaged idea or trend. Rather, mastering the art of gathering valuable ideas means training yourself to uncover interesting ideas across multiple sources and become diligent about collecting them.

TIPS & TRICKS: HOW TO GATHER IDEAS

- **Start a Folder** – A folder on my desk stores handwritten ideas, articles ripped out of magazines and newspapers, printouts of articles from the Internet, brochures from conferences and just about any other paper-based ideas I find interesting. This folder lets me store things in a central and highly visible way. You might choose to create this folder digitally, or use both. Either way, the important thing is to have a centralized place where you can save ideas for later digestion.

- **Always Summarize** – When you are collecting ideas on an annual basis, it is easy to forget why it seemed significant in the first place. To help jog your own memory, get into the habit of highlighting a few sentences, or writing down a few notes about your thoughts on the article. Later, when you are going through your gathered ideas, these notes will be useful in recalling what originally sparked your interest.

- **Seek Concepts, Not Conclusions** – As we learned in Chapter 2, a key habit of good curating is the ability to be fickle. In practice, this means not getting too hung up on the need to quantify or understand every idea you save in the moment. Many times, the best thing you can do is to gather something, save it, and then move on to the rest of your daily life. Perspective comes from having time and patience.

Step 2—Aggregating

Aggregating involves taking individual ideas and disconnected thoughts and grouping them together based on bigger ideas.

Once you have begun diligently gathering ideas, the next step is to choose a time to go and combine the early results of your observation and curiosity with thoughtful insights about what it means and how it fits together.

When you move from gathering to aggregating, you are taking the first step toward adding meaning to stories and ideas. One method to help you start is to use exploratory questions. Some of my favorites to try are listed in the "Aggregating Questions" box below.

1. What broad group or demographic does this story describe?

2. What is the underlying human need or behavior that this idea is an example of?

3. What makes this story interesting as an example?

4. How is this same phenomenon affecting multiple unrelated industries?

5. What qualities or elements make me interested in this story?

At this stage it is important to remember that industries or categories don't matter for grouping. When sorting, don't fall into the obvious trap of putting all the financial examples together or putting every story related to Facebook together.

Aggregating involves sorting ideas based on insights and human motivations, not industries or demographics.

When I was preparing my *2012 Non-Obvious Trend Report*, I collected marketing stories of new campaign strategies from three different companies, Domino's Pizza, Ally Bank (an online consumer bank) and Aviva (world's sixth largest insurance provider). The industries across these examples ranged from banking to food services to insurance.

The shared lesson behind each of their efforts though was how companies were finding new ways to avoid being faceless and find their humanity, so I aggregated them together in a group and wrote on an index card "companies being more human."

In this second step, it is not important to come up with a fancy name or even to do extensive research around any stories. Instead, you want to start building small clusters of ideas which bring together smaller concepts into broader groups to be analyzed later.

- **Focus on Human Needs** – Sometimes focusing on a bigger underlying human emotion can help you see the basis of the example and why it matters. For example, the basic human need for *belonging* fuels many of the activities people engage in online, from posting social comments to joining online communities. The more you are able to connect the ideas you have gathered with the basic human needs behind them—the more easily you can start to aggregate ideas.

- **Recognize the Obvious** – Along the path to uncovering non-obvious insights, there is some value in recognizing and even embracing the obvious. In a grouping exercise for example, you can often use the obvious ideas (like multiple stories about new wearable technology products) as a way of bringing things together and work later on finding the non-obvious insights in between them.

- **Follow Your Intuition** – When you train yourself to be more observant, you might also find that you start to develop a feeling for stories that somehow *feel* significant or fit together even though you may not be able to describe why. Embrace that intuition when it tries to surface a connection between ideas without the words to describe it. In later phases, you can think further about connecting these pieces into a more thoughtful trend concept.

Step 3—Elevating

Elevating trends means thinking about the underlying themes that relate one group of ideas to another to describe a single broader idea or shift.

If you have gone through gathering and aggregating ideas—this is the point where you will probably confront the same problem I do every year.

There are too many possibilities.

When I go through my annual exercise of curating trends, the first time I aggregate all of my ideas it usually yields between 70 and 100 possible trend topics. That is far too many for a book and a sign that there is more work to be done.

In this third step, the aim is to start to take a bigger view and aggregating multiple groupings of information together into something that might eventually be a trend.

ELEVATING QUESTIONS—How to Think Bigger about Ideas

1. What interests me most about these ideas?
2. What elements could I have missed earlier?
3. What is below the surface?
4. What is the bigger picture?
5. Where is the connection between ideas?

This can be the most challenging phase of the Haystack Method as combining ideas can also lead you to unintentionally make them too broad (and obvious). Your aim in this step therefore must be *elevating* an idea to make it bigger and more encompassing of multiple examples.

For example, when I was producing my *2014 Non-Obvious Trend Report* in March of 2013 I came across an interesting healthcare startup called GoodRx, which had a tool to help people find the best price for medications. It was simple, useful and the perfect example of an evolving shift toward empowering patients in healthcare, which I wrote about in my fourth book *ePatient 2015*.

At the same time, I was seeing retail stores like Macy's investing heavily in creating apps to improve their in-store shopping experience, and a suite of new fashion services like Rent the Runway designed to help people save time and money while shopping.

On the surface, a tool to save on prescriptions, and an app for a department store and a crowdsourced tool for renting dresses don't seem to have much in common. I had therefore initially grouped them separately.

While elevating trends, though, I realized that all of them had the underlying intent of helping to *optimize* a shopping experience in some way. I ultimately called the trend *Shoptimization*, to describe the many new mobile apps and startups designed to help consumers optimize the process of buying everything from fashion to medical prescriptions.

In the next step, we will talk about techniques for naming trends (and the backstory behind the term *Shoptimization*), but for now my point in sharing that example is that elevation is the step in the Haystack Method where you can start to make the connections across industries and ideas that may have initially seemed disconnected and fallen into different groups.

I realize the difference between aggregating ideas and elevating them may seem very slight. In fact, there are times when I manage to do both at the same time because the act of aggregating stories together may help you to broaden your conclusions about them.

In the Haystack Method, I chose to still present these steps separately because most of the time they do end up as distinct efforts. With practice though, you may get better at condensing these two steps together.

TIPS & TRICKS: *HOW TO ELEVATE AGGREGATED IDEAS INTO TRENDS*

- **Use Words to Elevate** – When you have groups of ideas, sometimes boiling them down to a couple of words to describe them can help you to see the common themes between them. When I was collecting ideas related to entrepreneurship for my 2014 report, for example, a word that kept emerging was "fast" to describe the growing ecosystem of on-demand services for entrepreneurs. It was the theme of speed that helped me to bring the pieces together to eventually call that trend *Instant Entrepreneurship.*

- **Combine Industry Verticals** – Despite my own cautions against aggregating ideas by industry sector, sometimes a particular trend ends up heavily focused in just one sector. When

I see one of these clusters of ideas predominantly focused in one industry, I always try to find another batch of ideas I can combine it with. This often leads to bigger thinking and helps to remove any unintentional industry bias I may have had when first aggregating ideas together.

- **Follow the Money** – With business trends, sometimes the underlying driver of a particular trend is focused on revenue generation for the businesses using it. Following this trail can sometimes lead you to make connections you might not have considered before. This was exactly how studying a new all-you-can-read ebook subscription service and the growth of cloud-based software led me to my 2014 Non-Obvious Trend of *Subscription Commerce*. Both were examples of brands transforming their business models to rely on subscriptions instead of sales.

Step 4—Naming

Naming trends involves describing an elevated idea in an easily understandable and memorably branded way.

Naming trends is a bit like naming a child—you think of every way that the name might unintentionally be dooming your idea (or child) to a life of ridicule and then you try to balance that with a name that feels right.

Of course naming trends also involves the choice of sharing a specific point of view in a way that names for kids generally don't. Great trend names convey meaning with simplicity—and they are memorable.

For that reason, this is often my favorite part of the Haystack Method but also the most creatively challenging. It is focused on that critical moment when you have the ability to craft an idea that will either stick in people's minds as non-obvious or be forgotten.

Sometimes this quest to share non-obvious ideas leads me to invent an entire concept.

My second book which focused on how likeability is the key to success in business is a perfect example of this. It was called *Likeonomics* and immediately became a business best seller the week it was released.

Back in 2006, I published a blog post on how content could be optimized for social media sharing. I called it *Social Media Optimization* and gave it the acronym of SMO. The idea spawned over a dozen SMO services companies still in business today and even has its own entry in Wikipedia.

Finding the right name for an idea can do that. It can help a smart idea to capture the right peoples' imaginations and help them to own and describe it for themselves. Of course, that doesn't make it easy to do.

In fact, naming trends can take just as long as any other aspect of defining or researching a trend. In my method, I try many possibilities. I jot down potential names on index cards and compare them side by side. I test them with early readers and colleagues. Only after doing all of that do I finalize the names for the trends in each of my reports.

NAMING QUESTIONS—
How to Ensure You Have an Effective Trend Name?

1. Is the name not widely used or already well understood?

2. Is it relatively simple to say out loud in conversation?

3. Does it make sense without too much additional explanation?

4. Could you imagine it as the title of a book?

5. Are you using words that are unique and not overused or cliché?

6. Does it build upon a popular theme or topic in an unexpected way?

So how do the names turn out? Of course, you could see the list of trends in Part II of this book to compare some of the trend names I developed for this year's report—but here are a few others from previous reports along with a little of the backstory behind the development and selection of each one:

- **Brutal Transparency (2011)** – Playing off the common phrase of being "brutally honest" the naming of this trend was meant to illustrate how brands were taking transparency to a new and unexpectedly extreme level as a way to build trust with their consumers.

- *Precious Print* **(2013)** – In an increasingly digital world, this trend was aimed at describing how more and more of us have come to place an even higher value on those things that we read or choose to print because we value them enough to bring them out of digital form. The word "precious" seemed like the perfect way to describe this sentiment, and also worked well alliteratively together with "print" to complete this trend's name.

- *Obsessive Productivity***(2014)** – As the life-hacking movement generated more and more stories of how to make every moment more productive, I started to feel that all of these tools and advice about helping each of us optimize every moment was bordering on an obsession. The naming of this trend was easy, but to me it worked because it combined a word most people associate as negative (obsessive) with a play on one that is usually discussed as a positive (productivity).

While there are literally dozens of ways to name trends, the following tips and tricks share a few of the techniques that I tend to use most often in naming and branding the trends in my reports.

TIPS & TRICKS: *HOW TO CREATE POWERFUL NAMES FOR TRENDS*

- **Mashup** – Mashups take two different words or concepts and put them together in a meaningful way. *Likeonomics* is a mashup between likeability and economics. *Shoptimization* is a mashup between shopping and optimization. Using this technique can make an idea immediately memorable and ownable, but can also feel forced and artificial if not done artfully. There is a reason I didn't call my book *Trustonomics*. Mashups should be easy to pronounce and as close to sounding like the original words as possible. Both *Likeonomics* and

Shoptimization sound like the words they are derived from, which makes them less likely to feel forced or over the top.

- **Alliteration** – When naming brands, this technique goes back to Coca-Cola or Krispy Kreme. The idea of using two words beginning with the same consonant is one I have used for trends like *Partnership Publishing* or *Co-Curation*. Like mashups, it can feel forced if you put two words together that don't belong, but the technique can lead you toward a great trend name.

- **Twist** – The technique involves taking a common idea or obvious phrase and inserting a small change to make it different. My favorite 2014 example is a trend I called *Over-quantified Life*. This was inspired by the growing topic of "quantified self" used to describe the world of fitness trackers and real time data on everything from our exercise to our sleep. The overquantified life trend was a way of using a term that was already in the public consciousness and then giving it a little tweak to help it stand out and get attention.

Step 5—Proving

Proving trends is the final step in ensuring that there are enough examples and concrete research to justify why an idea does indeed describe the accelerating present enough to be called a trend.

Up until this point in the process of developing and curating trends, you might be thinking there hasn't been much hard research involved. In the process I have shared so far, that is true. But it doesn't mean that data or hard research isn't important.

The Haystack Method relies heavily on analyzing stories and ideas that have been collected over an extended period of time and spotting patterns in those ideas. When it comes to proving a trend idea, though, getting the right research and data can be a critical last step.

In part, the amount of data and original research you might require depends on how you are looking at using the trends. The more analytical or scientific your stakeholders and audience, the more likely it is you will need some more concrete data to support your curated trends.

Regardless of what type of supporting trend research you intend to use, the proving method I use is focused on making sure that every trend has proof in three critical areas: idea, impact and acceleration.

WHAT IS A TREND?

A trend is a unique curated observation
of the accelerating present.

3 ELEMENTS OF TRENDS

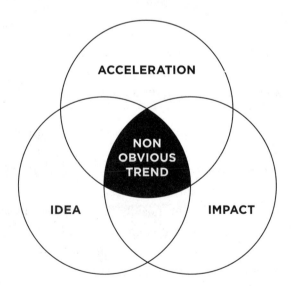

Let's look at each of these three elements in detail.

1. **Idea** – Great trend ideas are unique descriptions of a shift in culture, business or behavior in a concise enough way to be meaningful without being over simplified.

2. **Impact** – A trend has impact when it causes people to start changing behavior, or companies to adapt what they are selling or how they are selling it.

3. **Acceleration** – The last critical element of great trends is how likely they are to continue affecting business and consumer behavior into the foreseeable future.

For the past five years, these three elements have been the central filter I have used to measure my trend ideas and ensure that I apply the right discipline to making sure they are proven. One element of consistently doing this is asking the same types of questions every year to finalize my annual short list of 15 trends.

PROVING QUESTIONS—How to Quantify a Trend

1. Is the trend idea unique enough to be described as new or fresh?
2. Has anyone published research related to this trend idea?
3. Is the media starting to uncover examples or focus on it?
4. Are there enough examples across industries to show adoption?
5. Is it likely to continue into the foreseeable future?

As you go through these questions, you may notice that some of the trend ideas that you have curated, analyzed, elevated and even created names for may not satisfy all these criteria. Unfortunately, you have now reached the toughest step in the Haystack Method: leaving behind trends that don't work.

Abandoning ideas is brutal—especially after you have become attached to them.

It probably won't help that in this chapter I have already advised you to name them before you prove them—which seems logically wrong. You never name something you're going to leave behind, right?

Well, as true as that may be, the problem is that you often *need* to name the trends before you can truly realize their importance. The process of naming helps you understand what a trend is and how you might prove it.

And if you ultimately find that a trend doesn't particularly work, you *must* abandon it and move on. Great trends always have the right proof to support them in front of the people they are meant to influence.

TIPS & TRICKS: *HOW TO PROVE YOUR TREND IDEAS*

- **Focus on Diversity** – One of the quickest ways to uncover that a trend idea may not actually be a trend is if you are only able to find examples of it in a single industry, category or situation. For example, I remember several years ago considering the idea of "Short-Form Communication" as a trend because of the rapid growth of Twitter and texting but I couldn't find enough diverse examples to prove the trend, so I abandoned it.

- **Watch Your Biases** – Nothing will cloud your judgment more quickly than finding a trend that somehow helps your own industry, product or career. This is a tricky subject because part of the intention of curating your own trends may specifically be to support a product or belief. Yet it is also where many of the trends that are oversimplified or just plain wrong come from. Real trends, don't have apparent industry biases and are not gratuitously self-serving.

- **Use Authoritative Sources** – When it comes to the examples and research that you find to support a particular trend, the more authoritative sources you can find, the better. What this means in practice is using examples that people may recognize or finding research from reputable organizations or academic institutions. These sources can make the difference between selling your vision or having your audience question your conclusions because they don't believe your sources.

Whether your ideal method for proving trends involves relating them back to fundamental human needs or supporting your ideas with examples of successful businesses and quarterly revenue, there are many ways to prove a trend.

The trends you can predict with the Haystack Method are neither focused solely on consumer behavior, nor on global economies. Instead, this method can help you observe and identify patterns in media, culture, business or any other topic that may have particular relevance for you.

As a final step to help you put the Haystack Method into action, let's go through a step-by-step example of how it was applied, using one of the trends from this year's *Non-Obvious Trend Report*.

CASE STUDY:
How to Curate a Non-Obvious Trend

When writing this case study, I must admit I was tempted to take the easy way out and use a trend from one of my previous reports. Instead, I felt it would be more powerful (and useful!) to track my progress in real time as I developed one of the trends for this year's report, so I wrote this section simultaneously while doing research and writing the trend below.

The result is this section, which takes you through all five steps of the Haystack Method to gather, aggregate, elevate, name and prove a single trend from this year's *Non-Obvious Trend Report*. You can read more about it in Chapter 15, "Engineered Addiction."

THE TREND— ENGINEERED ADDICTION
STEP 1—Gathering

One of the earliest stories I saved, from February 2014, was about Dong Nguyen, the creator of mobile game Flappy Bird, which he suddenly pulled from the iTunes and Android stores after millions of downloads because he began to worry that the game was becoming too addictive.

His unexpected choice seemed significant—though I wasn't yet sure exactly why—so I saved it. Later that same year, I read a book called *Hooked* about how Silicon Valley product designers could build addictive "habit forming products" that seemed to describe perfectly what Nguyen had unintentionally done (and felt so guilty about)—so I saved that idea as well.

STEP 2—Aggregating

As I started the process of aggregating stories together from those I had gathered, I started seeing a pattern in stories that seemed to focus on some type of addictive behavior. The Flappy Bird story was about game design that seemed to lead to addiction. The book *Hooked*, by Nir Eyal, was about product design and using it to create habits in people.

To aggregate these together, I focused on the idea of design and the role that interface design seemed to be play in creating all these addictive experiences. I stapled these stories together to group them and put an index card on top with the simple description "Addictive Design" to describe what I guessed the trend might be.

STEP 3—Elevating

When I stepped back to look through my initial list of about 75 possible trends, there were several other trend concepts that stood out as possibly being related to this idea of Addictive Design. One in particular was an education-based trend I had started to track around the use of gamification techniques to aid in how people of all ages could learn new skills or knowledge.

I had used the relatively obvious term "Gamified Learning" on that index card to aggregate an article about the Khan Academy using badges to inspire learning and a startup called Curious that was making learning addictive by creating bite-sized pieces of learning on interesting topics.

The final piece to add to the puzzle as I was aggregating this trend was a book I had read back in 2013 called *Salt Sugar Fat* (by Michael Moss), which had also focused on the idea of addiction, but in the world of food manufacturing. The book exposed how foods like Oreos and Cheetos had been created to offer a "bliss point" that mimicked the sensations of addiction in most people. Along with the book, I also had several other articles on that topic saved under the term "Irresistible Food."

Adding the potential trend of Gamified Learning together with Addictive Design and considering the idea of Irresistible Food, I realized that there was an elevated trend that they all might be describing. This bigger trend described how all sorts of experiences and potentially all sorts of products as well were being created as intentionally addictive based on more than just design or interfaces.

I put all the stories for each of these three aggregated concepts together and called the elevated grouping "Ubiquitous Addiction."

STEP 4—Naming

Now that I had plenty of examples as disparate as food manufacturing and online learning, it was time to put the pieces together with a name that would describe this bigger trend. For some trends, a name I develop during either aggregating or elevating the trends might work for the final trend name. Unfortunately, in this case "Addictive Design" seemed too small and "Gamified Learning" was too obvious and niche. The elevated name I had quickly assigned, "Ubiquitous Addiction," also didn't quite work, and didn't exactly roll off the tongue either.

I needed something better.

The final clue as to what the name of the trend could be came from another interview article I read which featured Eyal, the author of *Hooked*. In the article, he was specifically talking about his belief that his role was one which he liked to describe as a "behavioral engineer." This idea of engineering instead of just design immediately seemed far better suited to describing what I felt the trend actually was.

After testing a few versions of using the word "engineering" in the title of the trend, I settled on *Engineered Addiction* as the most descriptive and memorable way to describe this trend and all of its components.

STEP 5—Proving

The final step was to ensure that this was truly a trend that could be proven through more than stories across multiple industries. In this case, the proof was already done, in large part through the exercise of research because I had uncovered so many dimensions to the trend in different industries across the previous steps.

I still wanted more proof, though, so I started looking for more examples or evidence of intentionally addictive products and experiences. My research led me quickly to a recently published Harvard Study showing why social media had become so addictive for so many, and then to a book by noted MIT anthropologist Natasha Dow Schüll, who spent more than 15 years doing field research on slot machine design in Las Vegas.

Her book, *Addicted By Design*, exposed the many ways that casinos use the experience and design of slot machines to encourage addictive behavior. Together, these were the final elements of proof that would help tell the story completely.

Engineered Addiction made my *2015 Non-Obvious Trend Report*, and is now Chapter 15.

Avoiding Future Babble

Now that we have gone through the method used to build out, describe and prove a trend, there is only one final thing left to do—offer a word of advice against one of the biggest dangers of trend forecasting: sinking into nonsense.

Despite my love of trends and belief that any of us has the ability to learn to see trends—the fact is we live in a world frustrated with predictions, and for good reason.

Economists fail to predict activities that lead to global recessions. Television meteorologists predict rain that never comes. And business trend forecasters are perhaps the worst offenders, sharing glassy-eyed predictions about future industries that seem either glaringly obvious or completely impossible.

At least 50% of pundits seem wrong all the time. It's just hard to tell which 50%.

In 2011 journalist Dan Gardner wrote about this mistake-ridden obsession with the future in his entertainingly insightful book *Future*

Babble. Part of his aim was to spotlight the many ways that experts have led us down mistaken paths and caused more harm than good.

In the book, he refers to the research of Philip Tetlock, a psychologist from the University of California's Haas School of Business. Over the span of years, Tetlock and his team interviewed all types of experts and collected 27,450 predictions and ideas about the future. They then analyzed these judgments from their many anonymous sources and concluded that "the simple and disturbing truth is that the experts' predictions were no more accurate than random guesses."

> *No matter how clever we are, no matter how sophisticated our thinking, the brain we use to make predictions is flawed and the world is fundamentally unpredictable.*
>
> Dan Gardner, *Future Babble*

The more interesting conclusion from Tetlock's research, which Gardner highlighted, was the wide disparity in how some experts reacted to the news of hearing their predictions were wrong.

The experts that fared worst were the ones who struggled with uncertainty. They were overconfident, described their mistaken predictions often as being *almost* right and generally had an unchanging worldview. In *Future Babble*, Gardner calls these experts "hedgehogs."

On the other side were experts who did not follow a set path. They were comfortable with being uncertain and accepted that some of their predictions could be wrong. Gardner called these experts "foxes" and described them as modest about their ability to predict the future, self-critical and willing to express doubt about their predictions.

His discussion of foxes versus hedgehogs gets to the heart of an important question that you might be wondering yourself at this point in the book. How do you know your predictions are actually going to be accurate?

The Art of Getting Trends Right (and Wrong)

You already know that I believe anyone can learn to predict the future.

Yet I also shared Dan Gardner's caution about the dangers of false certainty and general skepticism around future predictions for a reason.

If you are going to build your ability to curate trends, you also must simultaneously embrace the idea that sometimes you will be wrong.

In Part III and the appendices of this book, you will see a summary of every trend I have predicted in my last four annual editions of the *Non-Obvious Trend Report*. Each trend also has a corresponding letter grade and a retrospective analysis of its longevity.

Some of them are embarrassingly off the mark.

The reason I share them candidly anyway is partly to illustrate Gardner's point. I want to be as honest with you as I try to be with myself after each year's report. Foxes are comfortable with uncertainty and know they may sometimes be wrong.

I *know* I am sometimes wrong, and I guarantee that you will be, too.

So, why write a book about predicting the trends and go through this entire process if we both might be wrong at the end of it?

A fear of failure is no excuse not to apply your best thinking and explore big ideas. That's the first reason. The second comes to my true purpose in writing this book—which is only *partially* about learning to predict trends.

Learning to predict the future has an even more predictable side effect: you will become more curious, observant and understanding of the world around you.

It is this mental shift that may ultimately be the greatest benefit of learning to see and curate trends.

Oscar Wilde once wrote that "to expect the unexpected shows a thoroughly modern intellect." *Non-Obvious* is about building this type of modern intellect through seeing the things that others miss, thinking differently and curating ideas describe the accelerating present in new and unique ways.

Now that I have shared the process and techniques I use to do that every year, let's focus on my predictions for the top trends that will be changing how we buy, sell or believe anything in 2015 with the next edition of the *Non-Obvious Trend Report*.

PART II

THE 2015 NON-OBVIOUS TREND REPORT

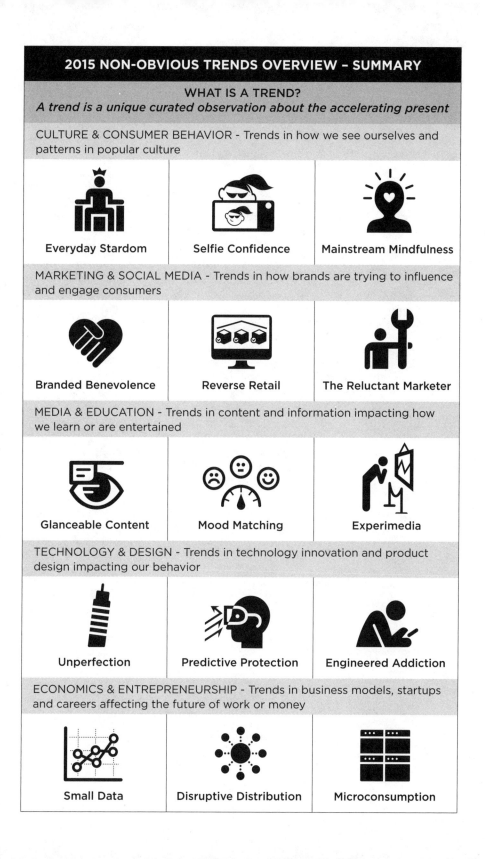

Chapter 4

EVERYDAY STARDOM

What's the Trend?

The growth of personalization leads more consumers to expect everyday interactions to be transformed into celebrity experiences with them as the stars of the show.

On the morning of November 15, 2013, most of San Francisco woke up with no idea that their city was about to be saved by a superhero.

The fact that this particular superhero happened to be less than four feet tall and was only five years old were details most of the city would only learn after his heroics would go viral for millions of people to watch unfold online in real time.

Months earlier as a kid being treated for leukemia, Miles Scott told the Bay Area chapter of the Make-A-Wish Foundation the one thing he wanted–to be Batkid.

To make it happen, a team from the nonprofit started preparation on a plan to get about 200–300 people to show up at City Hall to support a staged event where Miles could wear a costume as Batkid and defeat an actor dressed as one of Batman's longtime enemies.

It quickly became clear that they had far more interest than they expected.

A longtime video game designer signed on to help design the experience. A social media agency volunteered to help promote the event. And countless people started following the plan on Twitter and vowing to show up in person.

When November 15 finally came, an estimated crowd of 20,000 people showed up at City Hall to cheer on Batkid.

As watchers shared the day on social media with the hashtag #SFBatkid, a worldwide audience started paying attention. All told, the event generated more than half a million tweets, real time conversations in 117 countries and more than 16,000 photos shared on Instagram.

The day even prompted San Francisco Mayor Ed Lee to declare November 15 as Batkid Day and inspired a feature-length documentary about Miles' story called *Batkid Begins* which was released in January 2015.

Most importantly the day transformed a little boy's life and offered a moment that, as one spectator put it "restored your faith in humanity."

In a time when these types of promises are used as click bait in overly sensationalized media headlines, Batkid day stood out for being, as the documentary film promos put it, "the day the Internet was nice."

It turns out at around the same time Miles was having the best day of his young life, one of the largest entertainment companies in the world was rolling out a technology system designed to create a magical experience to give millions of kids (and the adults that came with them) the feeling of being superstars just like Miles every day.

Disney's Master Plan

The ambitious MagicBand and MyMagic+ initiative from Disney to transform the experience at their flagship theme resort in Orlando, Florida, was estimated to cost over a billion dollars. Affecting everything from how visitors book rides in advance to how resort rooms were accessed, the effort is one of the most ambitious to integrate wearable technology in the travel and hospitality sector.

A MagicBand is a waterproof wristband that can act as a room key, theme park ticket, mobile payment device and more. It also lets Disney collect a vast amount of data as visitors move around the parks, which helps the company manage crowds. Depending on how guests choose to set up their Disney accounts, the MagicBand also allows characters to recognize and address them by name (if they choose), and for Disney to create photo packages where families can build memories through automated albums of the many pictures taken of them throughout Walt Disney World.

Clearly Disney wants to offer a personalized experience to every guest, and they are not alone. This ambition to completely personalize a customer experience is one that many other brands—from established fashion labels like Burberry to startup custom bike seller Villy Bikes—are trying to integrate into their experiences.

The goal they all are working towards is at the heart of this trend of *Everyday Stardom*—to allow customers to feel like superstars with every branded interaction.

Bollywood Brides

While the idea of stardom may seem like a stretch at a theme park or when ordering a customized bike, it's far more understandable on the one day when most people might *expect* to feel like stars: their wedding day.

In India, weddings have taken such a central role in the culture that many of the best loved films from the country's vast film industry, known as Bollywood, feature weddings in almost every story.

The Bollywood industry collectively releases more than 1000 films every year (about double the output of Hollywood) and a favorite scene in many of them is the over-the-top musical wedding featuring colorful outfits, flash mob–style dances and melodramatic courting rituals filmed in scenic locales ranging from Swiss mountaintops to Brazilian beaches.

The prominence of this fantasized wedding tradition has recently led to a surge in the "matrimonial matinee," as the *Times of India* called it, where soon-to-be married couples hire a film crew to help them recreate these scenes from films as part of their wedding videos to share with guests.

Of course, part of the appeal of having a beautifully filmed and choreographed wedding video (whether ii features a Bollywood dance theme or not!) is the chance to share it with friends and family. Aside from our human desire to be the star of the show, a big motivation for wanting to create these types of stardom experiences is the chance to share it through social media with the people we care about.

Weddings don't happen every day, and for most of us they (hopefully!) only happen once. On your wedding day, you *expect* to be the star of the show. Now, you might come to expect it when you pay for a scripted experience like going to Florida to experience the attractions and magic of Disney.

What about every other day?

Me: The Museum Experience

In 2011 Intel launched one of the year's most successful social media campaigns, focused on a simple idea: to allow people to create and share a museum of their own lives. Luckily, the ideal foundation to build this already existed—on Facebook.

Attending events, sharing photos, posting interesting quotes or observations about daily life are all the types of content most people were already posting to Facebook. The concept of the Museum of Me was to create a tool you could apply to your Facebook profile to search your past posts and photos and arrange them into an interactive experience.

You could literally watch your life unfold over the time that you had been active on Facebook and share that story with your friends and family.

If you think about it, the concept of taking social data and using it to create a celebrity-like experience is one that we see almost every day on social media. Instagram users recreate celebrity poses in their own attempts to take memorable selfies. Twitter users share pithy observations to entice retweets, or simply find stars to follow and share their thoughts directly.

Social media and the rise of the personal brand enables consumers to put themselves at the center of their own life narratives, creating personalized moments and memories as a result.

Why It Matters

The beautiful human story of fulfilling a sick five-year-old boy's wish, the efforts of Disney to personalize your visit to their theme parks, Bollywood wedding videos and the rise of personal branding through social media all share a single underlying theme: the human desire for recognition.

Everyone wants to be noticed, recognized and celebrated.

Dale Carnegie once wrote "a person's name is to that person the sweetest most important sound in any language." His point, made through years of observation, was that people are hardwired to seek out moments of recognition where they feel singled out, understood and appreciated.

In a world where individualism is rising, the human desire for recognition can become paramount. When people want to feel like stars every day and have the tools and platforms to expect it—the leaders who connect and the brands that inspire loyalty will be the ones who offer personalized treatment, celebrate their consumers, and manage to treat them like the stars they long to be.

Who Should Use This Trend?

The most powerful element of this trend is how it crosses between leadership and business. Retailers and those who offer a physical experience will find this trend particularly valuable, however anyone in a leadership position should also consider the implications when it comes to leading a team and inspiring them to believe in a mission. This trend is equally applicable whether you happen to be trying to integrate more personalization to improve a customer experience, or trying to inspire more loyalty from a group of people you are trying to lead or influence.

How to Use This Trend

✓ **Ask personal questions** – Most of us have been taught that it is impolite to ask questions that are too personal. The problem with censoring ourselves against getting personal is that you may lack the information you need in order to really treat someone else like a star. Disney's MagicBand asks for an extraordinary amount of personal data, but they reflect it back to their customers in an obvious way that makes it useful. When you ask customers to share more, it can lead you to a valuable insight to help personalize an experience in a way they may remember for a lifetime.

✓ **Use data you already have** – One of the biggest ironies of many organizations is the store of data that has been collected but never used. Do you have your customers' physical addresses? If so, do you ever send them something proactively that isn't a marketing offer? The point is not to collect data simply to fill a hole in a spreadsheet. If you ask for a piece of information, be sure you're going to use it—or don't ask in the first place.

✓ **Focus on memories people can share** – One of the most frequently shared pieces of advice in business today is about creating experiences instead of selling products. It is good advice, most of the time. To effectively use the trend of *Everyday Stardom*, though, may require more effort not only on creating a memorable experience, but also on helping people to actually remember it by helping them share it as it happens.

Chapter 5

SELFIE CONFIDENCE

What's the Trend?

The growing ability to share a carefully created online persona allows more people to use social content such as selfies as a way to build their own self confidence.

What would you do if your most embarrassing picture went viral?

Caitlin Seida unfortunately found out, when her most embarrassing photo, of her at a Halloween party dressed as Lara Croft from *Tomb Raider*, went viral.

For weeks before she saw it, the photo had been making the rounds online—and commenters had been posting snarky comments about her choice to wear the costume despite being overweight. The cruel caption "Fridge Raider" had inspired hundreds of anonymously mean comments in response.

When she first found it, she was devastated.

It was the perfect example not only of the culture of nastiness that Internet commenting has become known for, but also of a technology-induced problem that has been accelerating so fast we have had to create a name for it: cyberbullying.

According to recent statistics from the i-SAFE Foundation, *more than half* of all adolescents and teens have been bullied online and about the same number have engaged in cyberbullying themselves. In response, there are a growing number of educational programs designed to help adolescents and teens deal with cyberbullying and even how to fight back.

When it comes to that fight, Seida's story has a positive outcome. Not wanting to hide from the past, and realizing that removing the image from the web was next to impossible, Caitlin Seida did that only thing she could think of; she embraced the embarrassment and told her side of the story.

On October 2, 2013, she wrote an article on Salon.com sharing her embarrassment at discovering the photo and also the fact that she had been having fun that evening and didn't regret dressing up as her favorite video game character.

She told her personal story of her medical struggles with polycystic ovarian syndrome and a failing thyroid gland, both of which caused her weight to spike. And she shared her story of confronting many of these commenters with a short message:

> You're being an asshole. Why don't you just do the right thing and delete the post and stop sharing it?

It takes self-confidence to stand up and confront a bully.

Thanks to the world of low privacy filters and an online culture of meanness and sarcasm—the ability to find new ways of discovering your own self confidence has become a daily necessity. The problem is, not everyone can find the type of courage Caitlin Seida did and channel it toward building (or rebuilding) their own confidence.

After the whole embarrassment faded, Seida did her own photo shoot with a retro pinup photographer and described the experience with these words: "that particular shoot felt great. Just to be seen a little bit more as I wanted to be."

That same sentiment underlies the rapid growth of the world's most unlikely tool for building self-confidence: selfies.

The Upside of Selfies

A "selfie" (as you have likely seen in the media many times) is essentially a photograph someone takes of him- or herself, usually with a mobile phone camera.

Earlier this year, while profiling a laughably popular product called the "selfie stick" (designed to allow you to extend a phone camera away from you to better compose your selfie), *Time* magazine noted that "if 2013 was the year in which *selfie* became a buzzword, then 2014 was the year selfies became a cultural phenomenon."

While that may be true, selfies certainly don't enjoy the greatest reputation as a *positive* cultural phenomenon.

Many people rate it the exact opposite, citing low attention spans, a rise in narcissistic behavior, and a temptation to use all those duck face poses and auto-filtered images to portray an unrealistic self-portrait.

In many ways, this usage of the selfie share a controlled version of ourselves is in response to the way the Internet has become a haven for the snap judgment "hot or not" types of rating and comments that can be so damaging to anyone's self-esteem.

Microsoft Principal Researcher danah boyd is well known for her aversion to the "self-righteousness" of capital letters (thus the use of lowercase to present her name throughout this chapter), and her years of work into understanding how young people use social media as a part of their everyday practices.

In her latest book *It's Complicated: The Social Lives of Networked Teens* (2014), she explores what the book terms as an online "culture of meanness and cruelty."

In her research, she explains this meanness as a natural outcome of the social world that teens must navigate, where attention has become a commodity. The ease of online commenting along with a media culture frequently critical of celebrities and personalities can even make this type of meanness seem normal.

In a world filled with anonymous meanness the real question is how teens (and many adults) can build enough self-confidence to be happy.

A selfie may be a greater part of the answer to that challenge than most of us realize.

Do Selfies Promote Selfishness?

The selfie has become the ultimate way to control how people see you online. Selfies can be posed, taken multiple times until they are perfect, and even filtered and corrected by retouching apps inspired by fashion magazine tactics to manufacture the ideal of beauty through their covers.

Just a few years ago, these artificially manipulated images of impossibly skinny models were generating a huge social backlash. Companies like Dove built viral campaigns designed to expose the reality of beauty and challenge each of us to question what it really means to *be* beautiful. In the process, "Photoshopped" became a dirty word as it began to describe the lie many consumers felt they were being sold by the fashion industry.

Now we can sell those same lies to one another and it doesn't seem quite so serious.

Instagram can instantly filter a sky to make that picture of a storm from your hotel window seem like an impending monsoon instead of a gentle afternoon shower.

An interesting question this led me to was whether this culture of online shallowness might also be part of the solution? Part of my answer came from what some might describe as the shallowest app ever created.

Facetune Yourself

The well-named Facetune app lets you take any image and immediately fix everything from whitening teeth to widening smiles and transforming cheekbones.

The site supporting the app features an entire tutorial on how to remove eye bags, acne and any other unsightly elements from your face before posting a photo to social media. The site has inspired plenty of other apps offering similar functionality as well.

The app offers understandable ammunition for those who joke that people who share too many selfies may be becoming "#selfieabsorbed." Selfies can easily seem like yet another example of the "me first" culture, focused on self promotion and little else.

Yet all of this attention on creating and sharing the perfectly sculpted selfies is having an unexpected side effect.

Selfies are becoming instrumental in raising self-confidence in those who need it most.

Why Selfies Are Good for Girls

In February of 2014, a new research survey of approximately 2000 adult and 200 teenage Americans from Today and AOL.com released a series of predictable results about how women and men view their own body image.

The study reported that women spend on average about 100 hours more than men per year on their appearance, and both men and women worry about being overweight.

Aside from an even longer list of "insights" like these, which are unlikely to surprise anyone, a single unexpected figure did stand out. While less than half of adults (40%) said selfies or other flattering photos online usually made them feel more confident, when this same question was asked of teenage girls, the number went up to 65%.

Around the same time, another article by author and co-founder of Girls Leadership Institute Rachel Simmons posed a similar theory with a far more direct headline: **Selfies are good for girls.**

If you write off the endless stream of posts as image-conscious narcissism, you'll miss the chance to watch girls practice promoting themselves—a skill that boys are otherwise given more permission to develop, and which serves them later on when they negotiate for raises and promotions. … A selfie suggests something in picture form—I think I look [beautiful] [happy] [funny] [sexy]. Do you?—that a girl could never get away with saying.

Not only was this an article in support of selfies as a way for teens to build confidence, but Simmons proposed the intriguing view that selfies might even be the secret to leveling the playing field between boys and girls as they started to approach adulthood.

Why It Matters

Our online identity is becoming a greater and greater part of who we are to the world. For virtual friends and others you rarely see in person, it is this selectively created sense of self that may even become the "real you" far more than the daily person in real life whom distant friends and relatives may rarely see. While this may seem like a scary deception, the good news is there is plenty of incentive for each of us to bring those two visions of ourselves closer together.

For most of us, it is not only easier to be the same person in both worlds—it is far more fulfilling. Leading a second life where your online persona is completely divorced from who you really are is increasingly the stuff of science fiction. Films love to imagine what this avatar like existence would look like.

In reality, though, the research shows we seem to be heading far more towards fact than fabrication when it comes to our online identities.

The Social Media Lab at Cornell University has published a series of interesting articles on topics as wide ranging as why college students seem to be less deceptive when creating LinkedIn profiles than they are when writing a resume, to why most Facebook profiles *do* reflect our authentic selves instead of some exaggerated version.

Rather than making us self-centered liars, studies show that social media may, over time, be giving us the one thing we need if we want to find and be ourselves: power over our stories.

Ultimately, the strength of the *Selfie Confidence* trend comes down to this simple principle. Selfies are not only symbols of the everyday control we now have to shape the story about ourselves we want to tell. They also offer us the support and permission to ultimately *become* that image we share online without pretending.

Who Should Use This Trend?

If you have an experience that you offer for people in real life, such an event or some type of retail store, this trend will clearly be valuable to think about in terms of how people can share that moment in a way that is likely to help them tell a story about themselves that has personal value. In addition, brands that are celebrated by their most passionate customers by appearing frequently as props or backdrops in selfies will have a huge opportunity to find and support their greatest evangelists through social content—if they know how to look for it.

How to Use This Trend

✓ **Overcome the Narcissism Bias** – The common criticism of selfies is that this newfound ability to be both the photographer and subject of the photograph is creating a generation of me-first monsters unable to empathize with others. If you don't fit into what some have called the "selfie generation" (as I don't!), it is tempting to condemn all those selfie sharers as shallow and narcissistic. To benefit from this trend, the first thing you must do is force yourself to avoid being closed minded about the potential value of selfies.

✓ **Leverage Photo Analytics** – If you are going to connect with customers who are featuring your brand in selfies, you'll need to find them first. Unfortunately, without text these images can be impossible to find. Thankfully, more software innovators like Ditto Labs are pioneering solutions to help scan photos posted online for everything from brand logos or fabric patterns to celebrity faces.

✓ **Make Experiences Easy to Share** – When food research firm Technomic published 10 restaurant trends that would take off in 2015, near the top of the list was the belief that a meal would become a "staged event that imparts bragging rights." This idea of staging real life experiences to share them is increasingly central to the experiences themselves. As a result, providing great Wi-Fi or interesting backdrops can help insert your brand or experience into content and selfies being posted by social media–savvy consumers.

Chapter 6

MAINSTREAM MINDFULNESS

What's the Trend?

Meditation, yoga and quiet contemplation overcome their incense-burning reputations to become powerful tools for individuals and organizations to improve performance, health and motivation.

In August of 2013 *ESPN* magazine published a story about the rise of mindfulness, meditation and yoga as training strategies in an unlikely place: the NFL.

The story went inside the unusual summer training camp activities of a team whose coach had decided that spirituality and well-being were going to be part of his team's pre-season preparation.

To prove his commitment, he hired staff dedicated to player well-being, including a life-skills counselor and a director of player development. In a sport defined by drill-sergeant coaching styles and "walk it off" toughness, even the team's coaching philosophy was different.

Instead of berating players for making mistakes, coaches used encouragement to help them learn and get better. The team even changed its philosophy on player recruitment, actively searching for players with a positive attitude, and even trading away superstar players if they weren't also committed to being great teammates.

In September, this was the ultimate forgettable, feel-good NFL story, written to fill empty magazine pages before the actual season started. Six months later, the story received a lot more attention, thanks to a stunning Super Bowl victory from the team it profiled: the Seattle Seahawks.

After that first victory, *The New York Times* published a follow-up article to the ESPN piece with the headline "Title for the Seahawks Is a Triumph for the Profile of Yoga." A year later, the Seahawks returned to the Super Bowl.

Thanks to the high profile of the sport, it certainly was a major victory for yoga and mindfulness in an unexpected place, but it is only one symbol of the major attention mindfulness is starting to get from multiple places.

The Silicon Valley Yogis

Mindfulness is widely understood and described as the state of being more conscious about yourself, your surroundings and those you interact with.

Being more mindful typically includes having more empathy for others, appreciating moments of quiet reflection and gaining a perspective that better allows you to manage stress or conflict when it comes.

Based on this definition, it is not surprising to learn mindfulness is often connected with yoga.

The growth of yoga in western culture over the past several decades has been dramatic. A November 2014 IBISWorld research report on Pilates and yoga studios, one of the few "recession-proof industries" of the year, projected an annual growth rate of 4.2% to 34,343 studios nationwide by 2019.

In California over the past year, Silicon Valley has also seen an explosion in meditation, yoga and mindfulness as a part of the daily work routine at tech companies of all sizes.

The one person who gets much of the attention for this growth is Google's head of mindfulness training Chade-Meng Tan. His official title is Google's Jolly Good Fellow.

A longtime Google employee (number 107), he spent many years trying to convince the company to implement more mindfulness training and exercises for team members. It took time, but they are finally listening. As Tan recently told *The Guardian*:

> *If you are a company leader who says employees should be encouraged to exercise, nobody looks at you funny. The same thing is happening to meditation and mindfulness, because now that it's become scientific, it has been demystified. It's going to be seen as fitness for the mind.*

Over a thousand Google employees have gone through programs as part of Tan's Search Inside Yourself training and the waitlist is hundreds long for others who want to get into courses. With topics like "Neural Self Hacking" and "Leading with Compassion," all this focus on inner reflection led a *Wired* journalist to conclude that across the Valley, "quiet is the new caffeine."

If that's true, its current barista may be Soren Goldhamer.

Seeking Wisdom

Every year Goldhamer hosts the popular Wisdom 2.0 Conference, which has a flagship event in San Francisco that routinely attracts over 2000 attendees from around the world interested in all aspects of mindfulness at work and in daily living.

The event has become a who's-who gathering of the tech industry mindfulness movement, with attendees from nearly every large tech company sending multiple employees to attend and partake in the combination of learning, meditation and conversations.

It is not the only large tech event to focus on the topic either. The World Economic Forum in Davos this past year featured 25 sold out sessions on the topic of mindful leadership, and Europe's largest tech event Le Web in Paris this past December featured discussions on the "Future of the Mind" as one of its top trends.

Given the popularity of mindfulness as a corporate philosophy in the tech industry, it is not surprising that there are a suite of new products designed to help take the sometimes elite promise of mindfulness and extend it more broadly.

Mindfulness Tech

Arturo Bejar builds social tools to help people be more mindful of each other and though he may not be a household name, it is almost certain that you interact with the results of his efforts on a daily basis. Bejar is a director of engineering at Facebook and is charged with what some have described as the toughest job anyone could have—to convince people online to be nice to one another.

In 2014, a *New York Times* profile dubbed him "Facebook's Mr. Nice," a job title that seemed to make sense given his work experimenting with tools to help reduce cyberbullying, and rewriting the network's alerts to be more compassionate.

Outside of Facebook, there is plenty of other innovation to create more mindful technology and products as well.

Thync, for example, is a startup with a solution *Business Week* described as "Silicon Valley's strangest new product in years," a Bluetooth-enabled "neurosignalling device" which uses electrical pulses administered directly to the forehead to create focus, instill calm and inspire creativity.

In other words, it is a device to let customers program their state of mind.

Thanks to advances in neuroscience and wearable technology, this type of innovation is becoming more and more commonplace. Outside of technology and Silicon Valley, the place where this mindfulness may be most promising is when it comes to the fields of media, education and learning.

Mindful Learning & Education

Andy Puddicombe has the kind of startup founder's story that you can't help sharing.

Longing for something different in his 20s, he became a monk and lived for 10 years in the Himalayas, Burma, India and Nepal. He came back with a mission to help demystify meditation and make it more accessible for people across the world.

Today his primary tool is the popular Headspace app, which offers a range of short and long guided meditation sessions from Puddicombe himself. The app has well over 1 million users in 150 countries around the world.

Learning mindfulness has also extended to education. The Mindfulness In Schools Project is a UK-based nonprofit that educates teachers on how to bring mindfulness into the classroom as a way to help students deal with the stresses of schoolwork, activities and bullying.

Last year the Snake River Correctional Institute, Oregon's biggest prison, even started a program inside the solitary confinement wing to use what they call a Blue Room with projected images of open landscapes and soothing outdoor scenes as a way to calm inmates and reduce violent behavior.

The innovation was named to *Time* magazine's "25 Best Inventions of 2014" list.

Why It Matters

Mindfulness and meditation are rapidly being integrated into everything from Silicon Valley tech campuses to Oregon's largest prison. While the popularity of yoga continues to grow, unlikely proponents of yoga and mindfulness like the Seattle Seahawks are encouraging a more mainstream audience to consider learning and practicing mindfulness for themselves.

As mindfulness goes mainstream, it will start to reach unexpected aspects of our lives and interactions with others. Facebook chats may subtly change. Work related brainstorms may be informed by this new perspective. Our relationships with one another may start to shift. In most cases this will be a good thing, as we treat one another with more empathy we can better communicate and understand one another as well.

With the trend, though, will also be the rise of naysayers who see it as foreign or too religious to be introduced into the most basic of institutions—such as government or schools. This debate will continue through 2015, as will the ranks of believers who share their own transformational stories of how mindfulness has changed their lives already.

Who Should Use This Trend?

As mindfulness shifts from an individual aspiration to an institution-based philosophy, anyone responsible for training or learning programs in an organization or company should watch this trend with interest. It has the potential to impact consumer behavior in terms of how we shop and which companies we align ourselves with. It also will impact leadership and team management as the "softer side" of business becomes a focus area. A final audience that may see great value from this trend is anyone in an overworked position or seeking more balance from the things they do for work and their own ability to relax and enjoy their down time with family or alone.

How to Use This Trend

✓ **Start with short bursts of mindfulness** – Meditation and yoga can seem intimidating to start. It is not always clear what to do and we can't all hire private instructors or visit yoga studios consistently. The good news is there are more apps and tools like Headspace that can help you start slowly. Another technique gaining popularity is to intentionally take a pause between meetings or activities for a set period of time in silence to reset for the coming activities of the day.

✓ **Seek out mindful moments for bonding** – In every team there are activities that relate to your daily work and those that can build a team. Most everyone wants to be part of a great culture, but fostering that type of culture means offering teammates a chance to bond over something other than the work. Conferences (like Wisdom 2.0) or live events can be great ways to inspire this to happen. If members of a team can experience significant mindful or meditative moments together, they are far more likely to connect on a deeper level and build trust in one another.

Chapter 7

BRANDED BENEVOLENCE

⊷

What's the Trend?

Companies increasingly put brand purpose at the center of their businesses to show a deeper commitment to doing good beyond just donating money or getting positive PR.

Toms Shoes has a chief giving officer.

Founder Blake Mycoskie is particularly proud of sharing this fact whenever he talks about the company that he was inspired to start back in 2006 after seeing struggling children in a village in Argentina who had no shoes to wear.

Toms is a fitting choice to start any conversation about brands doing good. While the idea of corporate social responsibility has been around for decades, Toms' well-known One for One program to donate a pair of shoes for each pair purchased is more than social responsibility.

At most large brands, efforts for the social good have been relegated to a subdivision of another low-priority department such as public relations or human resources. Despite donating millions of dollars to charity, the value of their efforts is often uncertain.

An ultimate example of this disconnect: in 2010 Facebook founder Mark Zuckerberg donated $100 million to New Jersey schools to help reform education. Nearly five years later, the effort has been widely criticized because the money went to expensive consultants and achieved little lasting educational reform.

Big challenges will always need big solutions, but the idea of a socially responsible brand today necessarily goes beyond donating millions of dollars. Consumers expect more commitment—and more stories of results.

At its core, the trend of *Branded Benevolence* focuses on the many ways that brands are now making a difference in our daily lives by through charitable deeds, employee commitments, and powerful media and storytelling that all go far deeper than simply donating large sums of money to good causes.

Can a Vending Machine Inspire World Peace?

One of the most popular digital marketing campaigns of the past few years was barely online, except for a short recap video posted to YouTube. Instead, the campaign went out into the real world as Coca-Cola installed "Small World Machines" in various locations across Asia.

The concept of this particular campaign was to place paired vending machines in two different locations, each featuring a video camera and interactive touch screen. In order to get a Coke from the machine, people on either end of the virtual machine would need to touch hands on a virtual screen and experience a "moment of happiness," as it was branded by Coke.

The emotion came from two sister vending machines—one in New Delhi, India, and the other in Lahore, Pakistan.

The video rapidly went viral as people celebrated the optimistic thought that a moment of happiness inspired by a vending machine could have the power to bring the world together—through a single shared moment between people from countries that had been longtime rivals.

It's easy to dismiss this campaign as yet another moment of commercial cleverness simply aimed at selling more soda from the most recognizable brand in the world. Certainly everything about the effort is perfectly on message for Coke, even down to the perfect little jingle at the end.

Coke has consistently devoted marketing dollars and creative efforts to this type of entertainment, which offers a bit of theater in a branded way, while also serving up a world-changing message of tolerance and togetherness.

It is a strategy that world leaders could do well to adopt as a way to change perceptions and perhaps even bring about real societal change in the process.

Of course, it's hard to imagine that geopolitical change is Coke's ultimate intention when doing these types of campaigns. Even so, social good as a tangential outcome is arguably just as effective as if it were the goal in the first place.

Perhaps this is even truer if it happens to *be* the intention, which was the case with another brand in mid 2014, when one of the most well-known entrepreneurs in the world chose to give away his company's biggest secrets.

How to Give Away Your Secrets

On June 12, 2014, entrepreneur Elon Musk stunned the technology and automotive industries simultaneously with a single blog post. On that day he announced that Tesla Motors would make hundreds of patents available to rivals and technology companies in order to accelerate the pace of innovation.

Far from being a risky business strategy, Musk's philosophy was based on the necessity for continued innovation, as he shared *Business Week*: "You want to be innovating so fast that you invalidate your prior patents, in terms of what really matters."

The announcement was a predictably huge victory in the media for Musk and Tesla Motors, but it was hardly the first example of a company committing resources to build an open source platform to move an industry forward.

Back in 2006, then-CEO of Sun Microsystems Jonathan Schwartz made a bold bet on the future of open source technology by committing Sun to an open source software business model rather than a hardware-based model. In the time since, other technology companies have also made similar commitments to open source models.

These technology commitments of Musk or Schwartz individually only represent moments in time or strategic moves to try and establish market dominance for a particular platform—yet they do create an interesting backdrop from which to consider the idea of this trend of *Branded Benevolence.*

In a world where it has become commonplace to see all kinds of large commitments to social causes, how have consumer expectations of what impact those brands will have on our lives or the world at large changed?

A growing body of research into the topic of how companies are impacting the world may have the answer.

Greater Expectations

In 2013, after 20 years of tracking American consumer attitudes towards businesses' involvement in social issues, consulting firm Cone Communications released a new report with a single conclusion: social impact was more important than ever. Their study found that 91 percent of consumers want to "see more products, services and retailers support worthy issues."

A Nielsen corporate social responsibility survey from 2014 found that more than half (55%) of global respondents said they are willing to pay extra for products and services from companies that are committed to positive social and environmental impact—an increase from 50 percent in 2012 and 45 percent in 2011.

As further proof, a study published by Accenture in June of 2014 titled "The Consumer Study: From Marketing to Mattering" surveyed more than 30,000 consumers in 20 countries around the world. An overwhelming 72% responded that they felt business was failing to take care of the planet and society, and that this was a problem.

The report ultimately went on to conclude that "today's citizen consumer has higher expectations of business; dissatisfaction may be the product of traditional approaches to sustainability, centred on philanthropy and CSR."

The conclusion is simple: people expect more from business today—and businesses need to respond. As the stories in this chapter illustrate, many of them are doing exactly that.

Rise of Conscious Capitalism

In January of 2013, Whole Foods CEO John Mackey co-authored a book about the growing necessity for something that was increasingly being termed "conscious capitalism" as a way to describe the practice of doing business with a conscience. In his book, Mackey takes readers inside the tough choices Whole Foods has been making to either to avoid selling something (thereby losing revenue) or choosing to pay employees more or provide better benefits (therefore increasing operating expenses).

Other retails brands have been announcing similar choices, from CVS pharmacy committing to not sell tobacco products to Starbucks committing to have 100% of its coffee ethically sourced by this year.

The bottom line is, as more brands build on this level of purpose, the challenge will no longer become how to integrate some sort of social good into the way a brand does business. Instead, in 2015 the real challenge will shift to who is best able to relay that story of benevolence in a powerful and emotional way to connect with consumers.

Why It Matters

For years brands in many industries have become adept at the idea of soft branding community efforts. This longstanding technique of having a brand as an invisible supporter and patron was seen as the ultimate way to support something without it feeling overtly promotional.

Brands once believed that if they were associated with a particular social good, people would not trust their efforts. Today brands can earn that trust through positive business models, benevolent acts of charitable good, socially responsible sourcing and even entertaining brand messages of togetherness.

It is building of this type of trust that makes the idea of *Branded Benevolence* so valuable. In 2015, more brands will realize that doing business in a socially responsible way is only half of the challenge. The second part is putting your actions front and center to show what you believe and why you believe it.

Who Should Use This Trend?

The idea of injecting more kindness into how an organization interacts with customers or does business is almost universally applicable for companies in any industry. In particular, this trend can make a big difference for brands that have existing social-good programs but are struggling to make them more strategic and integrated into something bigger.

How Can You Use This Trend?

✓ **Give time alongside money** – Nothing can doom a well-intentioned effort more quickly than only offering money without any other commitment. As consumers get savvier about tax-deductible promises, it is important to think outside the donation. How could your employees get involved with the cause? What else can you offer beside money? Answering these questions can help you add more significance and make your efforts more human in the process.

✓ **Make kindness a goal** – An important element to remember about *Branded Benevolence* is that the trend also goes far beyond social good. Coca-Cola donates millions of dollars to causes each year, but their most memorable effort, featured in this chapter, was essentially a marketing campaign with a bigger vision. Sometimes adding value to culture means sharing an important message in an entertaining and shareable way.

✓ **Offer unexpected sacrifices** – In 2014, several brands made high-profile sacrifices as a way to demonstrate their own benevolence. Tesla opened their patents to the automotive industry. CVS stopped selling cigarettes, despite a full-year loss of revenue estimated at nearly $2 billion. These brands illustrate that sacrifice can be a powerful way to demonstrate *Branded Benevolence*; you are choosing to give something up because you believe in something bigger.

Chapter 8

REVERSE RETAIL

What's the Trend?

*Brands increasingly invest in high-touch in-store experiences
as a way to build brand affinity and educate customers,
while seamlessly integrating with online channels
to complete actual purchases and fulfill orders.*

At the National Retail Federation's annual expo event in early 2013, the rise of "showrooming" was a hot topic. The term was first coined to describe how consumers would visit a physical store to see and try out a product, and then go online in order to purchase it (often from a different retailer).

The annual IBM Business Value Global Consumer Study released around the same time validated retailers' concerns. IBM's survey of 30,000 global consumers concluded that nearly 50% of all online purchases made by consumers followed from some type of showrooming.

The numbers alone were enough to cause a ripple of panic for any retailer making big investments in maintaining a bricks-and-mortar location and losing significant revenue to online sales. How could they fight back?

Several panels at the National Retail Federation expo offered some relatively predictable strategies, from investing in a competing ecommerce store to somehow improving the retail customer experience. Retailers at the show left knowing they had to do something or risk facing obsolescence.

A year later when IBM came back to present the results from the 2014 edition of the same report, the data showed an unexpected conclusion. Even though consumers were increasingly shopping online, the data showed that only about 30 percent of all online purchases *actually* resulted from showrooming, a drop from nearly 50 percent in 2013.

The study concluded that showrooming was no longer a top threat for retailers. How could consumer behavior change so dramatically within a year?

The truth was, it hadn't.

Instead, retailers were increasingly becoming smarter about engaging what the industry had already started to call an omnichannel approach to retail by creating a seamless online and offline experience for customers. Some even started calling this fusion of physical and digital retail a "digical" or "phygital" experience.

Buzzwords aside, 2014 was the year that many pioneering retailers started to evolve how their retail stores could create experiences that inspired more brand loyalty and affinity, increasingly without selling *any* products in the stores at all.

The Tech Showcase

Samsung has been particularly aggressive in trying to get consumers to try their mobile devices in a bid to fight back against Apple's growth in the smartphone market. To help, the brand launched the Samsung Galaxy Studio in New York's fashionable SoHo shopping district as a way to showcase products and innovations without actually selling them directly to customers (which still mainly happens through third-party retailers).

Intel took a similar step in 2014 by partnering with a retail space called STORY created by entrepreneur Rachel Shechtman as "a retail concept that takes the point of view of a magazine, changes like a gallery and sells things like a store." The store featured a showcase of wearable technology products using Intel's technology as a component.

Even the world's largest retailer is looking at the rise of showrooming as an opportunity to grow sales. During a recent interview, Walmart's president and CEO of Global eCommerce, Neil Ashe, promised that showrooming "is not a bad word at Walmart ... if people want to showroom, then we are going to be the best darn showroom in town."

As more brands consider using a retail space as a showroom to build brand affinity and educate customers rather than directly sell, they are also rethinking one of the most fundamental assumptions of traditional retail: that consumers want to walk out of a store carrying their purchase.

Magic Mirrors & Bagless Shopping

If an exec in charge of innovation at a large brand predicted that "a physical retail showroom will never go away" because people will always want to use all five senses when shopping—it's tempting to dismiss it as a perfect example of how short-sighted executives can be the slowest to evolve.

When that exec happens to be at a brand that has no retail showrooms and exists entirely online, it's worth paying attention to. eBay's head of innovation and new ventures, Steve Yankovich, is a believer in the power of the retail experience. At the new Rebecca Minkoff retail store in San Francisco, for example, his team has created the technology to power several interactive mirrors to help shoppers select fashions to try on and match. The aim is to merge the physical experience in store with the ability to have products custom ordered and sent home.

Back in 2012, UK-based supermarket chain Tesco launched several virtual supermarket kiosks that allowed commuters in South Korea (and later other places) to use their mobile phones to scan QR codes of products that could be delivered later to their homes.

In 2014, the brand took the next step by piloting a virtual reality shopping experience in Berlin where consumers would use Oculus Rift goggles to simulate a virtual shopping experience integrated with online ordering and delivery.

Each of these efforts provides an interactive retail experience without the inconvenience of having products in the way.

The $1 Million Lobby

When Andy Dunn, the founder of popular ecommerce fashion brand Bonobos, decided to sell shirts from the company's website, he also built several fitting rooms in the lobby of the brand's headquarters to allow customers to try them on. Within months they were on track to do $1 million in sales directly from the lobby and he realized the potential of having a physical presence to augment their online sales.

By the end of 2014, the brand had opened 10 shops across the United States with plans to add 30 more in the next three years. The vast majority of orders still come through the online system. Dunn's major insight from that lobby experience was that most of their customers (almost entirely male) usually didn't mind leaving a store without a purchase in hand.

It is the perfect example of a *Reverse Retail* experience: one that was designed to create affinity in store and inspire a purchase that could be completed online and fulfilled later.

This approach of merging the physical and digital experiences together is one that Ron Magliocco, global head of shopper marketing at ad agency J. Walter Thompson Worldwide, calls "living websites," where an increasing number of shops flip the traditional retail model and simply become showrooms.

"Why would a store today stock 500 slightly different cameras?" Magliocco recently asked in an interview, "that's what the Internet is for."

Why It Matters

For years when retailers talked about the promise of creating multichannel experiences for customers, it basically meant having an online site as a way to avoid losing sales to competitors while focusing mainly on sales through retail locations—and the numbers supported that choice.

In 2015 and beyond, the connection between physical retail experiences and online buying is starting to reverse itself. The real life experiences are tailored to deepen brand engagement, and offer something memorable and valuable. The purchase itself, and how it gets fulfilled, is increasingly moving to the online environment where the "endless shelf" allows retailers to provide exactly what consumers want, customized to how they want it.

Thanks to increasing speed and capabilities for home delivery, this entire process becomes more and more seamless for customers so they can have goods delivered almost immediately, enjoy them soon, and leave a retail store with a memorable and shareable experience rather than a shopping bag.

Who Should Use This Trend?

Clearly the biggest users of this trend will be retailers or brands that make a product sold through some type of retail channel who must think about how to create an engaging live experience. The real life theater of retail has become the sales engine for later conversion online. This is also a clear win for any company that helps retailers to create these real life experiences or offers some type of event based service or platform to help make the retail experience more interactive.

Beyond retail or products, there is also an implication to reverse the sales process for many other activities, such as getting hired for a job or even teaching a group of people a new skill. No matter what you sell, this trend should inspire you to flip the model for selling it to use real life experiences as a way to entice an online engagement and purchase.

How to Use This Trend:

✓ **Create your own Genius Bars** – The most visible inspiration of the *Reverse Retail* trend is certainly Apple's long-standing Genius Bar method of putting experts in the store to offer customers help with their products (which have been mostly purchased online). The reason this works is because people often want personalized help with technology—and love the experience when they are able to get it.

✓ **Pilot new technology** – One of the ways that fashion retailers in particular are trying to stay ahead of this trend is to find new pioneering technology to test in stores, using everything from "magic mirrors" to interactive touch screens with automated product ordering. Regardless of the technology, working with partners and experimenting with existing technology allows you to be innovative without the burden of building it yourself.

✓ **Embrace spectacle for marketing** – BMW Performance Driving School teaches driving and offers factory tours without ever selling any cars. Microsoft puts motion-controlled Xboxes in the middle of shopping malls to let passersby play or watch motion-activated games. Both tactics work because they offer a highly engaging spectacle that encourages consumers to consider a later purchase of a larger and more expensive car or video game console system.

Chapter 9

THE RELUCTANT MARKETER

What's the Trend?

As marketing becomes broader than just promotion, leaders and organizations abandon traditional silos, embrace content marketing and invest in the customer experience.

The death of marketing is greatly exaggerated on a regular basis.

On the list of the many shifts that have been projected to kill it in recent years are social media, consumer empowerment, ad-skipping technology and the list goes on. Yet for every doomsday prediction about its demise, marketing always survives.

It doesn't, however, have the luxury of surviving unchanged.

Near the end of 2013, the annual meeting of the Association of National Advertisers brought together top marketing executives from all types of brands. At the event, ConAgra Foods chief marketing officer (CMO) Joan Chow publicly wondered "if in five to 10 years whether we should be called chief marketing offices anymore. Consumers don't like to be marketed to. We should be thinking of ourselves as chief value officers."

Other executives shared a similar vision of the changing role of marketing as well. Beth Comstock, CMO at GE suggested that her job was much more similar to a chief growth officer and Walmart CMO Stephen Quinn offered the view that CMOs really need to be chief innovation officers.

Why were all these CMOs actively looking to leave their titles behind? A big reason is the broadening role of marketing itself.

Rather than being responsible for only the messaging and promotion of products and services, marketing is increasingly crossing the line into informing product development and research. Customer care and service is blending with marketing through social media engagement. Even the role of IT is shifting, as leading Gartner analyst Laura McLellan recently predicted that by 2017 CMOs will spend more on technology than CIOs.

On the surface, this may seem to create an inevitable contradiction. If the role of marketing is increasing, and marketing spending is growing, why are so many CMOs trying to rethink their titles instead of embracing the role of being the chief marketer?

The answer lies at the heart of the *Reluctant Marketer* trend, and it has everything to do with what we consider to be great marketing today.

Marketing is about getting consumers to learn about and fall in love with what you do. Increasingly it is being done through stories, word of mouth, conversations and the customer experience itself. As a result, promotion is less dependent on outbound communication and more on rapid word of mouth through connected consumers ready to share their brand experiences instantly.

In a world where experience is the marketing—what you say matters less than what you do and how you do it.

The First Brand to Kill Marketing

On July 1, the world's biggest advertiser officially killed marketing.

As part of a big reorganization at Proctor & Gamble (P&G), the marketing organization was officially renamed "brand management" and hundreds of marketing directors shifted titles to become brand directors instead. The change was deliberate, meant to describe the broader vision brand directors are meant to have over managing an entire customer experience instead of just promoting a product.

At P&G now, brand management breaks down into four categories:

brand management (formerly called marketing), consumer and marketing knowledge (covering research and insights), communications (mainly external and internal relations) and design.

The last big shift at P&G in the marketing world was back in the 90s when the brand killed the restrictive "advertising manager" title in favor of a broader marketing title. The fact that they are doing it again now puts the brand on the front lines of a broader industry shift toward redefining the role of marketing itself.

If the past of marketing was about spending money in order to try and build value and (sometimes) sell a product or service, the future is about nurturing an entire experience that connects with consumers so deeply they can't help but talk about it.

Luckily, this shift has found a perfect voice in what is currently one of the hottest growth areas in business itself: content marketing.

The Ultimate Reluctant Marketing Tool

Content marketing is based on the principle that if brands can make their marketing more useful and focused on solving problems or answering questions, then consumers will embrace it rather than block it.

Content marketing is the ultimate tactic for reluctant marketers.

Over-the-top "buy one get one free" promotional offers are replaced by "how to" style content helping someone learn to do something better. Insightful experts previously working behind the scenes at organizations can now take center stage as employee spokespeople adding value and answering questions.

All these shifts are leading to marketing that is more human, believable and trusted.

To meet this growing demand for high-quality content, simply shifting the focus of marketing teams isn't enough—the team itself needs to change. In 2015 brands will continue the shift that has already started happening, and they will increasingly hire former editors and journalists to produce high-quality media.

Dawn of Brand Journalism

This influx of brand journalists also contributes to the trend of reluctant marketers. As more professionals trained in the balanced and objective ethics of journalism enter into communications roles, there are two predictable effects.

The first, which gets plenty of attention, is that those professionals may be enticed to compromise some of the principles they learned and embraced in journalism school. Indeed this fear has led to many hand-wringing articles by traditional journalists speaking out against colleagues who choose to work with brands. The second effect of this shift is equally significant but gets far less attention.

When you bring more talented, ethical, well-trained content creators into the world of marketing, they will be able to produce better, less-biased content.

Journalists always aim to tell a great story, but they are also reluctant marketers by their very nature. The *story* is far more important than inserting a branded message artificially or making sure the logo appears in just the right place.

Great content can make marketing more meaningful.

Why It Matters

As the definition and practice of marketing broadens beyond promotion, marketers are increasingly encouraged to think bigger than traditional marketing efforts to bring value to their organizations. For example, today's CMO and marketing leader is increasingly managing the customer experience, simplifying and explaining the brand promise, generating growth and sales, investing in technology, inspiring innovation and attracting top talent.

The marketer of the future is not constrained by marketing, and increasingly takes on that marketing-centric title with reluctance. Instead, these well-rounded leaders are imagining more open, less promotional and more useful brand experiences that cross over from marketing into business operations and ultimately reinvent how customers experience products and services on every level.

Who Should Use This Trend?

This trend most readily affects anyone who is currently working in a marketing position or navigating their path as CMO of an organization. The world of marketing has always changed rapidly, but 2015 will be a defining year for the CMO within an organization and a moment in time for leaders to carve their own path for how they will evolve the role of CMO to suit their own skills and the companies they work in. A secondary audience for this trend is anyone who creates various forms of media and may never have considered the role in the context of marketing, but who may now increasingly be working with organizations to put their skills to work building compelling stories on behalf of companies.

How to Use This Trend

✓ **Focus on experiences instead of promotion** – For anyone who has been trained in marketing, other customer experience elements like delivery to service to sales may seem as though they belong outside of marketing. That is increasingly no longer true. Are you building content to help your customers use your products *after* they have already purchased them? The key is using these moments to focus on improving experiences which generate more positive marketing and word of mouth, instead of just trying to upsell more stuff. ✓ **Support broader team integration** – Many reluctant marketers will have a background in other disciplines, from operations to finance to documentary storytelling. These outside skill sets can add big value, so a key priority of marketing leaders is to create a workplace where these sorts of intersections and integrations become commonplace and allow an entire team to escape the traditional confines of their own roles and broaden their collective vision.

Chapter 10

GLANCEABLE CONTENT

What's the Trend?

*Our shrinking attention spans and the explosion of
all forms of content online lead creators to optimize
content for rapid consumption at a glance.*

When Johannes Gutenberg produced the first fonts for his printing press in the early 15th century, they were modeled in a black-letter style to mimic the handwriting of the time. Over the hundreds of years since, designers and printers have experimented with creating fonts based on the human form, geometry and even trends in art and literature.

In 2012, noted font design group Monotype worked with a team of researchers at MIT's AgeLab to study the impact of type design on what the study called "glance behavior," the type of quick display reading most often utilized by drivers when interacting with a car's dashboard. The study found that using "humanist" typefaces with open shapes, wider inter-character spacing and varying proportions could produce a 13% increase in overall response time among males taking the study.

Clearly, reducing glance time is potentially lifesaving in a high-risk activity such as driving. It turns out the same feature may also be critical for any content creator trying to contend with one of the most profound consequences of our information-filled world: the shrinking human attention span.

According to the National Center for Biotechnology Information, the human race crossed a significant milestone in 2013 when our average attention spans moved to only 8 seconds, from 12 seconds in 2000. By comparison (for dramatic effect), the report also noted that the average attention span of a goldfish was 9 seconds.

The effects of this short attention span can be seen in almost every corner of the media industry. Popular reality television programs use faster edits and shorter scenes to tell their stories. Sensationalized headlines on media sites across the web, inspired by sites like Upworthy and Buzzfeed, create irresistible click-baiting temptations like "you won't believe what happens next."

In a low-attention-span world, the media that wins is the one that can capture attention in a moment—no matter how fleeting that moment happens to be.

Snackable Content

Nobel Prize–winning economist Herbert Simon famously wrote back in 1977 that "a wealth of information creates a poverty of attention."

To solve this attention crisis, one technique innovative marketers have increasingly turned to is the idea of creating "snackable content." Content marketing expert Jay Baer describes this quest to create useful bite-sized content in terms of "giving away information snacks in order to sell knowledge meals."

Judging by the results of some of the most successful content marketing brands, the snack might actually be tempting enough *without* the meal.

Oreos is a perfect brand to illustrate. The brand captured kudos from the entire marketing industry for its perfectly timed tweet during the 2013 Super Bowl blackout: "You can still dunk in the dark."

Since that day, the brand has continually moved from one real-time campaign to another.

The "Daily Twist" campaign featured unusual daily animated images of Oreos to share online. The "Cookie vs. Crème" campaign pitted Oreo lovers against one another based on their favorite part of the cookie. A

Halloween campaign invited consumers to create their own "nomsters" that would be created through stop-motion animated Instagram videos.

As a brand, Oreos offers the perfect case study for the upside of creating snackable content that can be consumed in a glance and disappears within several weeks after the campaign is complete. After all, when you are solely focused on creating *Glanceable Content*, who cares about creating something permanent?

Your Response Is Predictable

Of course, all of this focus on disappearing content is a side effect of the algorithm-driven way that most of us consume content today. We see the latest blog posts, recent tweets and frequently liked Facebook status updates based on our preferences that are built over time.

As we consume newsfeeds instead of homepages, we invite a curated bubble of content that *New York Times* writer Natasha Singer dubbed the "online echo chamber" to describe a myopic Internet where every piece of content we each see is personalized to us based on our likes, views and interests.

It is easy for an algorithm to predict an emotional response if it already knows what you tend to get emotional about.

You may be wondering how important the idea of creating glanceable media is when you consider how often we search for the information we want rather than passively sitting back and letting algorithms serve it to us.

Sometimes we seek out information that goes just a little deeper than all this snackable content.

How to Do Anything—In 3 Minutes or Less

If you ask a company named Demand Media, deeper content is where the real money is.

For more than five years, the online media company has been focused on soliciting freelancers to create specific content based on what people are actually looking for online.

To make its formula work, Demand Media runs Google searches through its own algorithms to determine what people really want, and what doesn't yet exist online. Then they commission freelance creators to film videos and create other content to post online.

The resulting content features advice on everything from learning to ride a bike to removing undesirable bugs from a home swimming pool. No matter what the content, it tends to be indexed highly on search engines and therefore generates traffic.

Each day, like a factory, the company publishes thousands of pieces of content to answer every question someone is thinking or may have typed into Google at some point. It is perhaps the most intensely algorithmic approach to creating content *anyone* has ever tried—and it has been working.

Why It Matters

The combination of our shrinking attention spans and the ready availability of social media content means that it is harder to capture anyone's attention than ever before. In response, content producers are getting smarter about using headlines, content formats and techniques designed to capture interest and incite emotional responses.

Together, this focus on *Glanceable Content* means that anyone with a message to share cannot afford to ignore aspects of content creation that once were considered optional, such as metadata or powerful headlines. In the media world of 2015, building content from the beginning to capture immediate attention and deliver value quickly will be key—and the brands or content creators who fail to realize this will fade into the rapid obscurity of algorithms and newsfeeds adept at burying content almost as quickly as it is released.

Who Should Use This Trend?

The industries most readily affected by this trend are media and entertainment brands that rely on capturing our attention to offer knowledge or pleasure. This trend also expands widely beyond the media industries to any brand trying use content to gain visibility or sell a product. As content marketing continues to become a key tactic for all types of brands, the challenge to create *Glanceable Content* should be one that is used by all types of marketing and communications teams who are actively using content as a part of their sales process. In particular, it has implications for more complex or B2B brands who are used to creating in-depth content that may not be as easily consumed in a glance or be optimized enough to connect with this new consumer mentality.

How to Use This Trend:

✓ **Create valuable curations** – In a little over two and a half years, an email summarizing the day's news for professional women called theSkimm has quietly gained more than half a million subscribers. Founded by two 28-year-old entrepreneurs, the daily email offers a fresh take on the news with irreverent views, and boasts an impressive average open rate of 47% (compared with the industry average of 18%). It is a powerful example of how curating content can add big value.

✓ **Focus on headlines** – The trick that many of the more popular and sensationalized media sources today have mastered is the art of writing compelling headlines. While I rarely advocate following the same "you won't believe what happened next" style of *Curated Sensationalism* (one of my 2014 trends), it is critical to spend enough time to craft interesting headlines in order to entice people to engage further.

✓ **Reverse engineer content topics** – A key component of creating *Glanceable Content* is knowing what your audience cares about most. Using Google's keyword analysis tools or "most popular article" lists are great ways to uncover content ideas that may be valuable for your audience. Once you know that, you can create the most valuable content possible.

Chapter 11

MOOD MATCHING

What's the Trend?

As tracking technology becomes more sophisticated, media, advertising and immersive experiences like gaming or learning are increasingly tailored to match consumer moods.

If you have ever been challenged to decide on a paint color for a new room, you have likely learned all sorts of interesting facts about the psychology of color, like how red can raise your energy level, or yellow in a kitchen can stimulate the appetite and digestion.

What interior designers and psychologists have known for years is that colors in a room can have a dramatic impact on your mood. Yet the science behind this is inexact. Small changes in shades produce different responses in each of us. And moods can change in a moment.

Unfortunately, for many years approximation was the best anyone could do when it came to mood. Today, that is changing.

Moody Marketers

In early 2015, Apple quietly patented a technology that allowed them to collect a mixture of physical, behavioral, and contextual data in order to track a user's mood and emotional state. While contextual advertising is already a hot topic, the idea that Apple might be able to use facial features or heart rate to target advertising is significant.

It isn't, however, all that new. Back in 2012, Microsoft filed a similar patent around its then-new Kinect facial-recognition technology, which was launched as part of the Xbox gaming platform. Clearly the promise of mood tracking for advertising has been around for many years. So what makes it different in 2015?

Adobe product marketing lead Kevin Lindsay wrote an underappreciated but insightful piece on the company's digital marketing blog about the coming evolution of how marketers use mobile data to track consumer moods and why it may be important, ultimately concluding that using it may be a "no-brainer." But it will only delight consumers if it is used ethically:

> *These omnipresent mood gauges will look at your interaction with your chosen platform and device—how hard are you hitting the touchscreen, how quickly are you moving between apps or content pieces, are you clicking fast or lingering, and, of course, the who/what/where/when of it all: what time of day is it, where are you, and where have you been? Compound that with things like social media status updates, music selection, and content consumption, and discerning a user's mood suddenly seems like a no-brainer.*

This same challenge of inferring a user's mood from the information they provide is inspiring both Yahoo and Google to invest heavily in developing contextual search to read not only what you type into the search bar, but the latent emotion behind it that hints at what you *really* meant to search for.

In another example of this shift from early 2015, Yahoo announced that it was acquiring Aviate, a company that provides contextual app search and organization for mobile phones. When announcing the acquisition on stage at CES, Yahoo CEO Marissa Mayer explained the value by describing how the app "suggests music apps in your car, fitness apps in the gym ... deliver[ing] the right experience to you at the right time, instead of you having to search for it."

Moody Matching describes this shift overall toward more brands collecting and using data on consumer emotions and moods to power the experiences and content that is offered back to consumers in real time online. The potential for this trend goes far beyond marketing.

Moody Media

In the December 2014 issue of the journal publication *Computers in Human Behavior*, a team of researchers from the School of Communication at Ohio State University published the results of a fascinating study of mood tracking and social media usage.

The study invited 168 college students who were randomly put into a good or bad mood by being asked a series of questions and then being told their performance was "terrible" or "excellent" to create the desired mood.

Afterwards, these students were asked to look at the profiles of eight students on a supposed new social networking site called SocialLink. The profiles had been created with public ratings of career success or attractiveness. When they reviewed which profiles students choose to explore further, they unsurprisingly learned that most tended to open the profiles of people rated as attractive or successful. More interesting was the fact that participants who were put into a bad mood before taking the test spent significantly more time also viewing the less desirable profiles.

When interviewed about the results, study co-author Silvia Knobloch-Westerwick concluded that "one of the great appeals of social network sites is that they allow people to manage their moods by choosing who they want to compare themselves to."

This impact of mood on the type of media that people seek is an insight that more and more media channels are intentionally making use of—as they tailor stories and experiences not by categories of topics covered, but rather by the emotion that readers or watchers can expect to experience when seeing it.

Alongside hefty categories like politics and business, for example, the Huffington Post also has an entire section devoted to "Good News" and another helpfully called "GPS for the Soul."

The growth of categories like these, coupled with the easy access to tools like RSS readers and apps that can pull in content and create personalized virtual magazines mean that anyone can create their own perfect compilation of media to consume online, to fit their mood at that exact moment.

Moody Experiences

What impact does your mood and emotion have on learning and performance in games and challenges?

The answer is quite a bit.

Researchers have seen a connection for years, but 2015 will be the year where the intersection of technology and immersive experiences will finally allow for many new ways to take advantage of this fact. For example, Sony has been experimenting for years with game controllers for the PlayStation that can use things like skin response and sweaty palms to predict how frustrating or difficult a game might be. In theory, if the game became too difficult the controller might be able to adjust to your playing styles and mood to become easier in real time.

On the learning side, the Yale Center for Emotional Intelligence has been researching how people can develop their emotional intelligence for years. One of the signature programs from the group is the RULER approach, an initiative to "provide evidence-based programming that helps school communities integrate the teaching of emotional intelligence into everyday practice."

The newly launched Mood Meter app from the group—a 99 cent app that allows users to record their moods in any particular moment to help them recognize the impact of their own emotions on their daily lives—was named one of the "next big things" for New Yorkers to watch by *The Observer* in early 2015.

Why It Matters

All of this attention on the role of our emotions and mood on how we learn, play and consume media is leading to more innovation in how these moods can be tracked and measured. As more brands learn how to tailor content and experiences by mood, the idea of Mood Matching will become as important an element of an overall experience as topics, demographics or any other measure in use today.

The implication for anyone creating content, producing marketing or trying to inspire some type of learning is clear: moods must be managed and tailored to in order to ensure your message and experience makes it through and delivers the value you hope it will.

Who Is Using This Trend?

Right now this trend is affecting industries as varied as media and publishers to big brand advertisers. Rather than being only valuable for a certain industry, though, this trend offers an underlying lesson that is likely to be useful for anyone faced with influencing anyone else to buy, sell or believe anything. Moods cannot be ignored and the better you get at tracking them and tailoring your message, the more likely it is you will be able to stand out.

How to Use This Trend

✓ **Focus on mood priming** – A big conclusion from the research around how moods affect the way we think and behave is that the mood a consumer has coming into an interaction will likely affect their perception dramatically. As a result, priming your customers by focusing on the mood they first acquire when interacting with you is critical. In the real world, this is yet another piece of evidence that first impressions matter. In the digital world, you can also lose customers right away by not welcoming them in the right way or having a bad initial user experience.

✓ **Build content for moods** – When people consume content based on their moods, it should affect how you create that content in the first place. What this means for any brand looking to use content marketing is that it's worth considering not only the usefulness of the content, in terms of whether it answers a valuable question, but also whether it is tailored to the right mood. If a consumer is likely to be frantic when seeking the content, it needs to be calming. If a consumer is frustrated, then simplicity and humanity is key. Regardless, the point is content can be tailored by mood, and increasingly should be as well.

Chapter 12

EXPERIMEDIA

What's the Trend?

Content creators use social experiments and real life interactions to study human behavior in unique new ways and build more realistic and entertaining narratives.

It took speaker, thinker and futurist Santiago Swallow exactly 72 hours to change the way the world would think about social influence online.

On April 17, 2013 he was introduced to the world as "one of the most famous people no one has heard of" through a flattering profile on Quartz.com written by Kevin Ashton, the man who first coined the term *Internet of Things*. By that point, Swallow already had tens of thousands of Twitter followers, plenty of seemingly astute observations about the human condition shared as tweets and a website promoting his upcoming book on the topic of imagined identities in the age of the Internet.

As if that were not enough, his tiny Twitter thumbnail bio photo showed a ruggedly handsome Mexican American male who was also described (by his own website) as "one of the greatest thinkers of the Millennial generation." It wasn't until about halfway down Ashton's glowing introductory article about Swallow that you reached the real punch line: he wasn't actually a real person.

As a social experiment, Ashton had created Swallow's profile a mere three days before, purchased thousands of fake Twitter followers for him and set up a fake WordPress account behind all of it. The total investment for all these efforts came to a grand total of $68 and two hours of set-up time.

Santiago Swallow was followed by hundreds of real people, retweeted by others and even achieved a social influence Kred score of 754 out of 1000, as measured by a leading social influence tracking company at the time.

If a fictional persona like Swallow can fool so many people (and algorithms) so quickly, Ashton seemed to be asking what that says about the way that we measure influence today?

This is exactly the type of question that more and more content is posing online with *Experimedia*, the inventive new method of using social experimentation as a lens through which to tell a story or uncover an interesting aspect of humanity.

The Woman with the Photoshopped Face

There is no more interesting topic to test human perception than beauty.

The world is filled with clichés about how we each perceive beauty differently and there is well-proven cultural bias attached to what people generally see as beautiful. It was this second truth that inspired freelance journalist Esther Honig to launch an ambitious mid-2014 project designed to explore beauty on a global scale.

She sent a photo of herself to designers in 25 countries with this simple instruction:

"Hi my name is Esther Honig and I would like you to enhance this image [of me] using Photoshop. I trust you will take whatever steps you see necessary. Make me look beautiful."

The resulting images she got back varied widely as designers from Pakistan, Serbia and the Philippines each applied a different filter to the idea of beauty. The effort captured the attention of media worldwide thanks in part to a featured story on Buzzfeed with the glanceworthy headline "This Woman Had Her Face Photoshopped in Over 25 Countries to Examine Global Beauty Standards."

Her aim was to discover if a global beauty standard exists, but during a later interview with Vice.com, she ultimately concluded it ended up in "a special spot between self-reflection, social commentary, and photo journalism that [was] made for social media channels. ... [which] seems to be the future of how we interact and discover information."

This future also happens to be true even if the vision behind it isn't quite as noble as shining a light on global perceptions of beauty.

Can an Expensive Car Make You More Attractive?

In a story seemingly crafted perfectly for British tabloids, two teenage pranksters armed with a handheld video camera and a YouTube account decided to visit a college campus and test a theory every teenage boy has likely heard at some point: that a beautiful and expensive car can make you more attractive to women.

To test the theory, Andrey Smygov and Victor G decided to take turns filming themselves using a Bugatti Veyron exotic car as a backdrop to asking female university students if they would be interested in sleeping with them. Of the five women who they approached, only two declined, which helped the video go predictably viral on YouTube.

Around the same time of this prank, a UK-based dating app was running its own social experiment with a far more romantic concept.

Aimed at testing the theory that we can form a love connection with someone before we see their face, they staged a speed-dating event where all the participants agreed to wear paper bags over their heads throughout the evening.

Though the bags had cutouts for your mouth and eyes, the test was enough of a stunt to entice journalist Marisa Kabas, a Today.com contributor, to attend and write about her experience. While the story didn't end with her meeting a soul mate, it did offer a captivating experiment about whether love is actually blind and what might happen if we tested that belief.

Why It Matters

There was a time when social experiments were primarily conducted by students and professors working in psychology or anthropology departments at universities. We would hear the results of these experiments through research studies published in journals, or (if you weren't an academic) through the mainstream media simplifying and reporting on the results after they were published.

Today these social experiments are being launched with far greater frequency and resulting in interesting explorations of all aspects of humanity—and they are published by everyone from individual content creators and thinkers to brands looking for unique ways to engage audiences more deeply.

In the coming year, this style of *Experimedia* will be used far more consistently and dramatically to make a point or promote a point of view.

Who Should Use This Trend?

This trend has been used quite frequently by brands targeting beauty and health products, thanks to the highly visible efforts of Dove over the decade since launching their global "Campaign for Real Beauty." Outside of beauty and fashion, though, plenty of consumer packaged goods, alcohol and even financial services brands can realize value from trying to use this technique of *Experimedia* to create interesting and engaging content that people can't help but share. It is also increasingly used by independent content creators who are trying to build their own audiences to start careers in media and entertainment, or to build enough of an audience individually to get discovered by larger platforms.

How to Use This Trend

✓ **Visualize complex topics** – One of the most successful recent efforts using this trend was a series of ads from Prudential Financial produced in partnership with Harvard professor Dan Gilbert. The ads depict real-life visual experiments designed to motivate Americans to better understand and prepare for retirement. The brand's latest ad in the series involved toppling the world's tallest domino and setting a world record in the process. What it illustrates is that using visual experiments can simplify a complex topic and capture attention in the process.

✓ **Tell an emotional story** – In 2013, Dove crossed the 50 million-view mark on YouTube with its latest video in the "Campaign for Real Beauty." Like its previous efforts, Dove used a social experiment—this time a former FBI sketch artist drawing women's faces—in order to underscore the brand's message: "you are more beautiful than you think." The real life social experiment was so compelling, that delivered the brand message far more powerfully than a traditional ad.

✓ **Recreate experiments** – One of the nicest things about the rise of social experiments covered in the media is that you have plenty of ideas to pull from for when it comes to building your own experiments. While doing this well may seem like it requires an entire video team and a vast experience you may not have internally, launching your own experiments only takes curiosity and a willingness to engage people and freelance resources online who may be able to help with the details.

Chapter 13

UNPERFECTION

What's the Trend?

As people seek out more personal and human experiences, brands and creators intentionally focus on using personality, quirkiness and intentional imperfections to be more human and desirable.

Christian Rudder knows more about people than you do.

He's not a body-language expert or behavioral scientist, but he does have access to something that most of us never will: a treasure trove of data about what people find attractive about one another and what they don't.

Rudder is the founder of dating site OkCupid and for the past several years he has been writing a blog called OkTrends about some of the strange and quirky insights that have emerged from all of this data. On the blog, he writes about his small, data-based observations, like how religious people don't seem to care as much about using proper grammar and how most people seem to prefer dating someone from the same race they are.

Thanks to all this dating data, Rudder can also spot underlying trends in behavior that we may not always be able to see.

Around the recent launch of his new book *Dataclysm*, for example, he shared this insight with *BusinessWeek* magazine: "polarizing looks—people with unique features or lots of tattoos—get 10 percent more messages and dates than conventionally attractive people. A lot of people are put off by them, but the people who like them really like them."

In other words, we are attracted to people who are more unique and who stand out, even if they happen to be less perfect by traditional measures.

On the surface, this may not be that difficult to believe. Being polarizing helps you stand out—and standing out is usually a good thing when it comes to trying to capture attention through an online dating profile listed alongside hundreds of others.

This principle of us appreciating the imperfect extends far beyond dating, though. Particularly when it comes to a certain type of hideous clothing that sparked a strangely popular national holiday between Thanksgiving and Christmas.

Celebrating Ugly

Although no one really knows where or when the first Ugly Christmas Sweater party took place, the authors of the *Ugly Christmas Sweater Party Book* (yes, it's a real book) suggest that it was probably in Vancouver, Canada, more than a decade ago. The book itself played no small part in anointing the second Friday in December every year as Ugly Christmas Sweater Day, where people hold their own parties and invite guests to don their own ugliest sweater.

The day has become big business, with the NFL and NBA even jumping on the bandwagon and offering a line of team-branded ugly sweaters available for sale online just for the occasion. And for several years now, Bank of America has even been running national television ads featuring ugly sweaters as a new holiday tradition.

While these sweaters may be an example of something ugly becoming popular mainly in jest, some products are succeeding in the real world thanks largest to their intentional ugliness.

Ugg boots are an authentically and unapologetically ugly product. After decades of selling the unique sheepskin boot whose name was inspired by an Australian slang term for ugly, Ugg boots achieved major recognition in 2000 when Oprah declared on her show that she "LOOOOOVES her Ugg boots."

Since then, the company's boots have become an iconic fashion accessory worn by celebrities and ordinary people alike—and they are celebrated for their quirky and ugly look. Whether considering the rise of ugly sweater parties or a piece of footwear that has been celebrated in part for its ugliness, the idea that people can derive pleasure in the intentionally imperfect—even if it happens to be ugly—is clear.

Ugliness is one form of imperfection, but it is hardly the only kind that has started to gain popularity.

The Makers of Imperfection

Early in 2014, an article in *The Economist* magazine coined the term "artisanal capitalism" to describe a rise in businesses and individuals creating handmade products and leveraging a growing range of online marketplaces to sell them to one another. It was broadly connected to the Maker Movement: the idea that we now have more technology and tools to be able to make for ourselves things that we previously relied on mass production to create for us.

As 3-D printers start to make their way into homes and tinkering becomes a mindset, it is not hard to imagine a world where this type of person-to-person commerce is the norm.

When it comes to handmade or artisan-built products, imperfection has always been part of the value.

At the online craft marketplace Etsy, some of the most popular sellers list everything from sets of unusual buttons and charms to unique hair accessories and bows for babies. Each product may not be perfect, but you can be almost certain no one else will have anything like it—and that makes it desirable.

The Origins of Imperfection

Astute readers of my *2014 Non-Obvious Trend Report* may realize that this trend is quite similar to one called "Lovable Imperfection" that I had shared in last year's report.

In that report, I focused on the intersection of flawed yet authentic celebrities (like Jennifer Lawrence) and lovable bad-guy heroes (like Walter White from *Breaking Bad* or Gru from the *Despicable Me* animated films). Those were symbols, I argued, of our desire for imperfection, and we often reward that desire with our attention and emotional investment.

So what is the difference this year? Though subtle, I see the largest change in this idea of *Unperfection* as a move from how we bond with people and connect with them through their imperfections, to *Unperfection* as an ideal that brands, experiences and products are intentionally aiming to create.

This is true even if those creations have more to do with design and an actual product.

Wrong Theory

In September 2014, *Wired* magazine devoted an entire issue and cover to what editor Scott Dadich had come to describe as Wrong Theory.

The idea of intentionally making bad design choices was something he started to embrace when designing the magazine because it added something that he couldn't quite explain. A little orange bar on the cover, headlines at the end of stories, and overlapping text on images all became intentional design choices.

Why would one of the most respected magazines in the world take this type of gamble with reader's attention?

There is a delight in seeing something unexpected. Though plenty of studies have illustrated how humans (and babies) prefer symmetry and routinely rate it as more attractive, what Dadich uncovered through leaving convention behind was that there is beauty in the imperfect as well, and that beauty may be far more worthy of celebrating.

Why It Matters

We no longer live in a world where everyone must strive for perfection. In examples from artisanal product sales to how designers are increasingly approaching all types of projects, this idea of making purposefully flawed products, services and experiences as a way to make them unique and desirable is gaining traction. What it means for all of us is that the emotional and personal aspects of an experience that make it memorable may be the exact same ones that might previously have been considered imperfect. The challenge for any of us will be to let those types of moments and features exist and delight customers instead of being removed in each iteration of our own processes.

Who Should Use This Trend?

This trend is important for anyone selling a product or service that has many competitors with similar offerings. The challenge in any crowded marketplace is finding new ways to be unique and stand out. Focusing on *Unperfection* can help you to add more humanity to your products and services and help them to stand out for what they are or for how you describe them.

How to Use This Trend:

✓ **Remember, imperfect is different than broken** – Following the news that we throw 300 million tons of food away each year, the European Union declared 2014 the year against food waste. Following the announcement, French supermarket Intermarché created a series of posters featuring "the grotesque apple, the ridiculous potato, the hideous orange, the failed lemon, the disfigured eggplant, the ugly carrot, and the unfortunate clementine." The posters were a viral success and managed to encourage hundreds of consumers in several pilot locations to purchase this "disfigured" produce at a discount. The point is, sometimes we equate imperfect as being the same thing as broken or unusable, but as Intermarché illustrated, these perceptions can be changed—it just takes the right creative approach to do it.

✓ **Make it purposefully flawed** – When describing his insight for Wrong Theory, *Wired* editor Scott Dadich was sharing the idea that sometimes it may be perfectly acceptable to create something that is purposefully flawed. It is a sentiment that many food manufacturers certainly agree with; consider the rise in so-called artisanal foods, or McDonald's imperfect new Egg White McMuffin (versus the perfect "hockey puck" regular McMuffin). The idea is, if you can add the flaws on purpose to a product or experience, you can make it more distinctive and perhaps make it seem more natural as well.

✓ **Embrace your "flaws"** – For NPR listeners, radio personality Diane Rehm has one of the most easily recognizable voices on the air. Yet for many years she has suffered from a neurological condition known as spasmodic dysphonia, which affects the quality of her voice. Rehm's "unperfect" voice is part of her personality and charm, and it helps her stand out. Amongst a sea of perfect altos reading the news, her voice offers something different, and millions of loyal listeners reward her for it with their attention.

Chapter 14

PREDICTIVE PROTECTION

What's the Trend?

The combination of high privacy concerns with elevated expectations about the role of technology in our lives leads to more intuitive products, services and features to help us live our lives better, safer or more efficiently.

When it comes to short-term motivation, there is nothing better than getting a new wearable fitness tracker.

After getting my first one, I remember routinely taking stairs and trying to walk more to hit my arbitrary daily target of 12,000 steps. On those meeting-filled days when I was stuck at the office, I would lament only hitting about 4000 steps and promise myself to do better tomorrow. Yet each of these positive behavior changes I exhibited in my first several weeks had major drawback: I had to keep plugging the device into the phone in order to see the data it collected.

Unfortunately, my tracker didn't sync wirelessly to the companion mobile app, and that single added step made it less useful. In fact, I forgot to plug it in so consistently that I lost focus on logging my daily steps altogether. About four weeks after getting the tracker, I was tempted to abandon it completely. In fact I almost did, but one subtle little feature kept me wearing it.

This little feature allowed you to select an amount of "dormant" time where you could be sitting down before your bracelet would vibrate, warning you that it was time to get up and move around. I had set mine at two hours, so if I was at my desk writing and losing track of time, the tracker would buzz on my wrist and remind me to get up and walk around.

This "Idle Alert" was the best feature in the device, and it became my sole reason for wearing my activity tracker for months after that. Yet it was also easily the *least* sophisticated thing that the device was able to do.

What made this tiny feature on an expensive device so valuable for me?

After thinking about this odd behavior on my own part, I realized that the real value of the tracker wasn't from the sophisticated technology or all the features it had. Instead, the fact that the Idle Alert could warn me to change my behavior *proactively* without the need for me to do anything was far more valuable than any other feature.

In other words, wearable technology was only useful if it offered *Predictive Protection*.

Stealth Health

Almost anyone you speak with will say they want to behave in healthier ways. Of course, saying that and putting it into action are two different things. You know in your head that it is not a good idea to eat an entire bag of Doritos, but unfortunately when contending with a product that has been manufactured to be addictive (see *Engineered Addiction* in Chapter 15), and when trying to use logic to fight a natural human response, you will nearly always lose.

Relying on willpower alone makes is difficult for most of us adopt healthier behaviors.

The good news is that the idea of tracking and proactively protecting us from ourselves via technology has become a common reality of the wearable-tech market today. For example, you can buy a tracker to monitor your breathing and help you adopt better respiration (Spire).

Another product called the Lumo Lift can analyze your neck and spinal positions to warn you if you happen to be slouching and give you alerts to remind you to correct your posture.

Since the time of my early fitness tracker, almost any tracker you can buy will have inactivity alerts, and even alarms based on your sleep cycle to ensure you only wake up at an optimal time in between deep and light sleep.

As these types of monitoring devices become more commonplace, the opportunities for our clothes, jewelry and even our furniture to offer us predictive alerts to help each of us adopt healthier behaviors will continue—and expand outside the world of health as well.

Protecting Our Driving

Whoever said that the shortest distance between two points is a straight line obviously never drove in rush-hour traffic. It is this type of traffic, and every driver's quest to avoid as much of it as possible, that has led to the dramatic growth of traffic tracking app Waze, which was acquired by Google in 2013 for the hefty sum of $1.15 billion.

Waze is a community-led mapping app where users (called Wazers) actively edit the maps in real time to share insights about traffic patterns, accidents, road closures and other factors affecting a particular route. Using Waze while driving can predict the optimal route and help you redirect to choose alternate routes when needed to optimize your drive.

In early 2014, Google Maps even added a feature likely inspired by Waze to suggest routes that were "5 minutes faster" or "8 minutes slower" via real time calculations each time you approach a fork in the road or encounter multiple potential routes to your destination.

Automakers are also adding more and more technology to predictively protect us inside of our vehicles while we navigate the riskier elements of driving. Already, blind-spot monitoring and lane-change assist are standard features on many cars, and forward-thinking tech companies are experimenting with self-driving cars.

Thanks to this growing range of features, entrepreneur and academic Vivek Wadhwa has already predicted that "in fewer than 15 years, we will be debating whether human beings should be allowed to drive on highways." As each new year brings more technology into cars, and it's not hard to imagine Wadhwa's forecast coming true at some point in the not-too-distant future.

Outside health and driving, the final industry that has been most affected by this new trend of *Predictive Protection* is the banking and financial sector.

Protecting Our Finances

In 2013 there was a new identity fraud victim every two seconds.

That was the worrisome conclusion of the *2014 Identity Fraud Study* released by Javelin Strategy & Research, which reported an increase of more than 500,000 fraud victims to 13.1 million people in 2013, the second highest number since the study began tracking fraud.

By October of 2014, the Identity Theft Resource Center was reporting 621 total large-scale data breaches, exposing a total of nearly 78 million consumers. Clearly, our data is not being protected very well—and consumers are worried.

To help take back control, a host of new online monitoring services and apps are allowing consumers to manage their own financial data and identity in more proactive ways. Card Control, for example, is an app that connects to your credit cards and allows you to selectively turn them on or off to prevent unauthorized use at specific times.

Banks issuing credit cards are also putting new technology in place to connect your identity with your cards, and even enable mobile payment options with the right authentication (which is generally far more difficult to steal).

Each of these are extensions of the already *Predictive Protection* that banks offer in terms of helping to keep your identity secure, your transactions free from fraud and your account up to date.

Why It Matters

The more data we share online, the more exposed we become in terms of the information about us that could be captured and used in unexpected or unwanted ways. Becoming more literate in how to protect our data is certainly important, but innovation in technology is leading to a growing number of apps, tools and services that can proactively protect us from these privacy invaders—and sometimes even from ourselves.

New innovations in wearable technology are helping to proactively make us healthier and change our behavior. Technology in and around the driving experience is making the process of getting from one place to another faster *and* safer for each of us. When it comes to finances and managing our money, tracking software and new tools can alert us of identity thieves trying to use our information in fraudulent ways.

These examples all point to the next generation of technology not only helping us to do things better and faster, but also to offer us *Predictive Protection* against negative situations, fraud and all types of unsafe behaviors to help alert us or even to correct them in real time.

Who Is Using This Trend?

The industries using this trend tend to overlap with the ones who are collecting the most ongoing data, and that fact has value. After all, offering *Predictive Protection* comes down to having the right data and then creating a way to consistently use it in a way that adds value for your customers or users. This data does not need to be proprietary, however. Other industries like athletics and retail also have many customer situations where there could be a benefit to creating *Predictive Protection* for customers through anticipating the likely hurdles in their customer journey and solving them proactively.

How to Use This Trend

✓ **Reprioritize Your Features** – When you think about the different features or benefits of your product or service, it seems logical to list the most significant elements first. Yet as my story of using a fitness tracker illustrated, sometimes the feature you think is the most useful isn't most valuable to your customer. Instead of listing and promoting your features in terms of significance, what if you listed them in order of *proactiveness*? In other words, the features that make your customers' lives easiest and require them to do nothing would be the most important and everything else would be secondary. Considering that might change how you promote your products and services, and understanding how can help you offer exactly the type of protection your customers are looking for.

✓ **Let Them Set It and Forget It** – One of the reasons that subscription commerce models work so well is because they allow consumers to, as Ron Popeil would say, "set it and forget it"—which essentially means that once they are subscribed, many of them won't remember or take the trouble to unsubscribe at a later time. Though this can be somewhat sneaky as a marketing strategy, the point is people want ease of use without the need to continually come back and modify it. Let them do this, and they are more likely to stay loyal.

Chapter 15

ENGINEERED ADDICTION

What's the Trend?

Greater understanding of the behavioral science behind habit formation leads to more designers and engineers intentionally creating addictive experiences that capture consumers' time, money and loyalty.

At the end of every year, Google releases an annual report that looks back over the previous year and shares some of the top trending topics people searched for worldwide. Most years, the top performing topics are fairly predictable. In 2014, the top three topics globally were Robin Williams, the World Cup and Ebola.

It was the entry that came in at number five on that list which was the most surprising.

Searches for Flappy Bird, an addictively simple game developed by a then-unknown Vietnamese game designer named Dong Nguyen, ended the year more popular than global events like the 2014 Olympic Games in Sochi, Russia.

Why was an obscure game with 1990s-style graphics so popular?

It turns out the biggest search spike came in February of 2014 when Nguyen decided to remove the game from the iTunes and Android app stores because he feared the game was too addictive. It was this addictive quality, and the unprecedented move of removing a popular (and profitable) game from iTunes that inspired hundreds of media stories trying to deconstruct the phenomenal success of Flappy Bird, and wondering aloud whether removing the game may have been a secretly brilliant strategy to create even more demand for it.

Among the circles of game and interface designers, the more interesting questions were not about the theatrics of Dong's release and removal of the game. Instead, the most compelling question was why the game was so addictive in the first place, and whether that type of addiction could be recreated.

Creating Habit-Forming Products

One of the most prominent voices digging into the science of what he calls "behavior engineering" is consultant and Stanford University lecturer Nir Eyal. His latest book, *Hooked*, explores the art of building habit-forming products and introduces the idea that anyone building a product can intentionally aim to make it a habit by following a specific process that he terms the Hook Model.

The idea that addiction to a product or experience could be engineered (and recreated) is a popular topic. Stanford has even invested in creating a *Persuasive Tech Lab* to explore the reasons why we become motivated, engrossed and loyal to certain experiences and not to others.

All of this research into reverse engineering addiction by design is also leading some observers and willing participants to ask tough questions about the true value and ethics of engineering this type of addiction.

In an opinion piece on tech site Gigaom, behavioral designer Jason Hreha dramatically likened all of this focus on building habit-forming products to being "the addictive equivalent of cigarettes—irresistible cheap thrills that feel good in the moment, but are destructive in the long run."

Even Eyal cautions readers of his book against using his Hook Model as a recipe for manipulation. Along with learning the power of manipulation, he argues, comes the responsibility of using it ethically.

Unfortunately, not everyone chooses to use the power of creating addictive experiences responsibly.

Addiction for Evil

About a year before Eyal published his guide to building habit-forming products, two books published within six months of one another tackled the subject of addictive products with a far more negative lens.

The first was a book called *Addiction By Design*, by an MIT Professor and cultural anthropologist named Natasha Dow Schüll, who spent 15 years doing field research studying slot-machine design and player behavior at these machines in Las Vegas. In her book she explores how slot machines today are engineered to be addictive through everything from the continuous rapid wagering of electronic interfaces to the surrounding experience providing ergonomic seating, minimal required arm movement, and cash-free betting via player cards with magnetic strips.

The numbers support her conclusions, as most industry estimates say that anywhere from 75% to 85% of a casino's total overall revenue could come from slot machines. In terms of number of people affected, though, the gambling industry is hardly the worst offender when it comes to using engineered addiction. That honor belongs to the food industry.

About five months after Schüll released her book, Pulitzer Prize–winning investigative reporter Michael Moss published *Salt Sugar Fat*, an inside look at the techniques food manufacturers had been using for centuries to mass produce products designed to offer addictive eating experiences.

Through a combination of taste testing and isolating the perfect balance between sweetness, saltiness, bitterness, crunch and many other qualities related to "mouth feel" of a product, food engineers have become adept at creating food products that are impossible to resist.

Almost every list of the most addictively engineered food products feature the same well-known American snack brands: Oreos, Cheetos, Goldfish crackers, and dozens of other products. What Moss writes about is the inside story of just how deliberately these products have been manufactured.

Together, these books paint a compelling picture of the evil side of *Engineered Addiction* which is important to discuss. However this trend is not always negative. There are important ways that this trend can be used to create something valuable and necessary.

The Upside of Addiction

The Khan Academy is perhaps the most celebrated education startup in the world.

With more than 5000 originally created videos on topics ranging from math to medical education, the nonprofit has generated plenty of excitement and belief for its ability to "flip the classroom" and allow students to learn complex topics at home through step-by-step videos.

There is an element of the Khan Academy, though, that has likely inspired more of the site's success than any other—even though it is far more rarely discussed.

When the site first launched, the founders knew that incentives would be critical to entice learners to make a bigger time investment. So the Khan Academy launched with a series of badges that users can earn for all sorts of behaviors on the site—from successfully mastering a topic to donating time to review a student's work.

You may be familiar with this method as *gamification*, and there are plenty of prominent voices who believe in its ability to help make learning addictive. One of them is Xprize CEO and entrepreneur Peter Diamandis, who devoted an entire chapter in his book *Abundance* to how technology is poised to impact education by helping to teach our children about the big picture of *why* the things they are learning matter. It is this combination of incentives, rewards, and meaningful learning that ultimately results in creating that sort of addictive experience that makes kids (or adults) want to learn anything.

Why It Matters

We often hear or see addiction treated as a negative force—used to describe everything from smokers' inability to quit, to viral gaming apps people spend far too many hours playing. When that addiction is designed to happen on purpose, it may seem even more evil. Yet, even though *Engineered Addiction* certainly has its negative examples, there are also applications, like gamified learning, where this design theory can be used toward a positive outcome.

Across industries as diverse as product design or architecture, this idea of engineering addictive experiences, products and spaces is increasingly being applied intentionally to increase engagement and results. The challenge with this trend, perhaps more than with any other, is to be among the leaders using it for positive outcomes rather than evil methods that encourage people to continue unhealthy behaviors, or waste their time and money.

Who Should Use This Trend?

Game designers have plenty of advice on how to leverage this trend, but any product design team or group responsible for creating a user interface will find the principles of this trend very useful. Information, education and learning organizations should also consider the lessons of this trend, in particular how to leverage some of the techniques that other industries such as gambling or software are actively using already.

How to Use This Trend

✓ **Reward engagement** – Loyalty programs reward engagement, and that same framework may be useful for building an addictive experience as well. Whether you use points, badges or some other type of incentive—the key is making these rewards visible and emotional enough that people will continually keep coming back for them.

✓ **Cater to a common human emotion** – Online learning website Curious.com features compilations of short videos on subjects like how to curl your hair and how to play the ukulele. The site is filled with snack-sized content, with high-quality videos and the promise of quick learning that happens so fast you are tempted to try another and another. The temptation and motivation is inferred perfectly by the URL of the site: curiosity.

Chapter 16

SMALL DATA

What's the Trend?

As consumers increasingly collect their own data from online activities and the Internet of Things, brand-owned big data becomes less valuable than immediately actionable small data collected and owned by consumers themselves.

In early 2015 more than 160,000 attendees descended upon Las Vegas for their annual trek to the world's largest tradeshow: the Consumer Electronics Show.

Most years, the increasingly slim televisions and consumer gadgets like tablets, phones and laptops get most of the attention, but 2015 was different. While the media still featured beautiful curved new TV screen designs and innovative new phones, there were also many unexpected products being featured.

There was a hair brush that holds an iPhone to allow people to take a selfies, a Wi-Fi–connected tea kettle for boiling water from your mobile device, and a smart tennis racket to improve your game. When you put these together with the growing range of wearable fitness trackers and technology embedded into our clothes, all of them are examples of the Internet of Things, where everyday objects become connected and collect data.

ECONOMICS & ENTREPRENEURSHIP

What is even more interesting about all this data is who owns and benefits from it—and who doesn't.

For years the Internet has been filled with places to voluntarily contribute our personal information in exchange for making things work. Want to buy a ticket to an event or download a "free" report? Trade your email address. Need to register a product? Answer a short survey to activate your warranty.

The more time we spend browsing websites, adding products to our carts, or sharing and publishing opinions through social media, the more this data is becoming part of the big data set companies can collect and use to customize product offers and market to us.

Influenced by growing consumer concern about how this data was being used (or misused), many governments have now created new regulations requiring data to be portable. In 2010 Facebook implemented a system that would allow every user to have more control of their own data, what is collected, and how they can export it and take it with them if they choose to delete their account.

For the first time in the world of privacy, data is co-owned by consumers *and* brands—a fact that is about to explode with the Internet of Things.

The Internet of *Your* Things

The Internet of Things is widely described as the ability for physical objects to be connected with wireless networks in order to integrate software, use data or be controlled remotely.

While this may seem like a popular buzzword, the category of products it describes is exploding as everything from wearable fitness trackers to smart thermostats are becoming more widely available. The single biggest theme that emerged from CES in 2015 was the importance of this data feedback loop from our products back to ourselves.

We are moving from simply being the creators of data through our behavior to the real-time consumers and owners of our own data.

This has big implications for your business in 2015.

Most of the discussion about big data usually focuses on a single theme: how companies can analyze and use the vast amounts of data they are now able to collect in order to create better, more personalized experiences for customers.

What if consumers could choose to share the data they have collected in order to improve their experience?

Consumer-owned *small data* is starting to rival brand-owned big data, and the key will be finding ways to link them together to create more value.

As data is increasingly unbundled, vast new self-created data sets will belong to consumers, created by those seemingly silly products like Wi-Fi tea kettles and mood-tracking bracelets. They now also have the keys to unlock this data from the platforms where it is collected and can choose to share it in ways that can benefit them. It's just not that easy to do yet.

If consumers could be enticed to share this data more easily, businesses could also unlock its power to augment their own data collection and create unheard of new customized promotions and products. This is not about the products themselves, but rather the nuanced, personal, and granular detail they are letting consumers collect about themselves and their own habits.

In fact, collecting this type of small data may be becoming an art form in itself.

Data Only *You* Can Love

When Ian MacLeod became a father, he did what almost any proud new dad might, take photos of his new baby boy. Unlike most dads, though, MacLeod kept on taking them, one per day, for 21 years straight. In 2012 he published a six-minute YouTube video montage featuring more than 7500 pictures of his son Cory growing from a baby to a 21-year-old man.

The video quickly went viral and currently has more than 6 million views on YouTube at the time of publication for this book. It is a perfect example of the power of consumer-created content, and the high emotions often attached to it, and it is also an example of small data.

Small data is often so personal that is has little intrinsic value to anyone except the collector.

Rather than simply being content, though, these collections of data often allow each of us to derive timely useful insights about our lives to make meaningful changes to our behaviors in real time.

As IDC analyst and vice president Mike Fauscette recently shared, "big data is useless, or even more than useless because it can distract businesses and consume a lot of resources for no value return. Big data can be made smart data if it can be made smaller, by transforming it to become contextual, relevant, and delivered to the right person at the right time, in the right format."

There are many dedicated to trying to solve this challenge.

One of the most well known is professor Deborah Estrin. Once described by *ComputerWorld* magazine as one of the "unsung women of technology," in the past several years Dr. Estrin has been recognized on a global level on CNN's "10 most powerful women in tech" list and *Wired* UK's "Smart List" of 50 people who will change the world.

Accolades aside, her current work in the Small Data Lab at Cornell University focuses on the growing collection of personal data we are each creating in every moment as we navigate the Internet, use our web-enabled devices and explore the world physically and virtually. These activities are offering a unique glimpse how we behave and also how we each may be changing our behaviors in response to our own self collected data.

The Usefulness Of Small Data

It is this ability to immediately act that stands out as the greatest benefit of collecting small data. It may not be able to help you draw broad conclusions about an entire population or demographic, but it is dramatically good at helping solve a short-term challenge. There are some who believe this may be the only type of challenge actually worth solving with data.

Rufus Pollock is the founder and co-director of the Open Knowledge Foundation and a frequent critic of those who overstate the value of big data. Instead, he believes that small, linked data is far more valuable:

For many problems and questions, small data in itself is enough. The data on my household energy use, the times of local buses, government spending—these are all small data. Everything processed in Excel is small data. When Hans Rosling shows us how to understand our world through population change or literacy he's doing it with small data. This next decade belongs to distributed models not centralized ones, to collaboration not control, and to small data not big data.

In a recent opinion piece for the Huffington Post, Brian Kibby, who has a background in learning technology and publishing, wrote about a similar idea in the world of education.

His point centered on the fact that small data focused on how students actually learn and perform is far more valuable than big data about their macro spending habits, location information, or medical and dietary information. Small data, in other words, is immediately useful in a way that big data isn't.

Why It Matters

The explosion of devices connected to the Internet and social media platforms that allow people to capture every thought or memory instantly mean we are producing more data than ever. Most of this data is not solicited, or traditionally owned by brands, which creates a new model of data ownership.

Consumer-owned data rivals brand owned data, and the biggest question facing any business in the coming year is how consumers will or won't choose to share that data. Small data is the term that emerged over the past few years to describe the value of immediately actionable data versus broad, complex and historical big data.

As we move into the coming year, the ownership of data and how easily it can be shared and acted upon will become the ultimate economic metric for whether data ultimately provides new insights and real value or just remains collected on vast servers and databases as its value slowly expires.

Who Should Use This Trend?

Though big data sometimes seems like the domain of large brands and governments, small data is accessible to any of us, whether you happen to be a blogger trying to optimize your own website, or a small business collecting customer feedback through surveys. The key will be to combine a smart approach to capturing and reviewing only the data that matters, then with finding new ways to act upon your customer's personal data if they choose to share it with you.

How to Use This Trend

✓ **Offer to use consumer-owned data** – Just because a consumer may be collecting their own data and you don't have an easy technological method to download it doesn't mean you can't benefit from it. For example, if you own a sports and fitness store, you could ask consumers to bring in a printout of some of their self-collected wellness data in order to help them select better products. The point is, there are many ways to use customer data, whether you can download it or not.

✓ **Watch for new popular products** – One of the lessons from CES that may offer interesting opportunities for you is to track what products are starting to take off and gain widespread adoption. As more people put a smart thermostat like Nest in their homes, it may open more opportunities to speak with them about energy conservation. If your business is in this space, the adoption of this type of product can open new doors. Similarly, there may be other products coming that could affect your industry, if you can make sure you are watching for them.

Chapter 17

DISRUPTIVE DISTRIBUTION

What's the Trend?

*Creators and makers use new models for distribution
to disrupt the usual channels, cut out middlemen
and build more direct connections with fans and buyers.*

There are two things I learned about Taylor Swift this year: she believes that the music industry is not dying and her apartment smells like an Anthropologie retail store.

The source of her views on the music industry is fairly well known. In early July 2014, about a month before releasing her single "Shake It Off," she published an opinion editorial piece in the *Wall Street Journal*, where she shared her optimistic vision for the future of music.

My inside knowledge of her apartment comes from a tweet shared by an adoring fan who was among the chosen few Swifties (Taylor Swift's biggest fans) invited back to her NYC apartment for a pizza party after the live online launch show for her new song.

While Instagram and Twitter were flooded that night with shares and reshares of images from that pizza party, journalists and music industry analysts were hard at work trying to figure out what this all meant for the future of the industry itself.

Complicating matters was a string of disruptive releases by well-known artists distributed directly to their fans.

About six months earlier, Beyonce famously delivered the release of an entire album without any advance promotion in a single night, including videos for each song. In an interview after the launch, she described her motivation behind releasing the entire album simultaneously by saying "that vision in my brain is what I wanted people to experience."

This desire and ability to connect directly with audiences and displace the middle men has expanded beyond music as well.

Unbundled Entertainment

Comedian Aziz Ansari released his latest comedy special, *Dangerously Delicious*, directly to fans via online platform VHX.tv, following Louis C.K., who made more than a million dollars in his direct release's first 12 days.

Outside of individual stars, even television networks and cable channels are starting to use direct distribution as a way to remove their reliance on networks for distribution.

In October 2014, HBO announced it would be selling a version of HBO directly via the Internet in 2015. CBS, the only broadcast network that is not part of Hulu, announced soon after that "CBS All Access" would provide web-based access to all the channel's programming.

Each of these examples is a natural result of the growth in fast Internet access and devices that can stream media entertainment. Aside from the growth of streaming, though, is an important secondary effect of this form of media delivery ... a more direct connection between creators and consumers without gatekeepers to control the price or access.

In industries where there are relatively rigid structures to create near monopolies of distribution, this type of disruption is increasingly becoming commonplace. Most of the examples above focus on forms of entertainment, but *Disruptive Distribution* is affecting many other industries as well.

The Death Of Academic Journals

In early June 2014, online publishing site Academia.edu passed the impressive threshold of signing up its first 10 million users.

For most of these academics, the method for sharing valuable research has been the same for decades. After conducting research, the typical path for publishing is to submit to an academic journal, which then provides an authoritative peer-reviewed process to validate the research and then publish it to the industry.

Not only has this model for publishing been in practice for decades, but it also generates billions of dollars for a select few publishers who own the vast majority of the journals, including Elsevier ($3.2 billion in revenue for 2012) and Springer ($1.1 billion for same year).

It is estimated that both companies have margins higher than 35% thanks to their exorbitantly high costs of subscriptions and relatively minimal cost of content production (since researchers or reviewers are rarely paid).

Price's aim with Academia.edu is to transform this industry by offering a viable alternative.

Though his greatest challenge lies in offering a viable alternative to the reputational value that the current journals offer, as the size and continued usage of the platform continues—the site offers a clearly valuable alternative to the closed distribution ecosystem of academic journals.

Dealership Wars

If the definition of an industry pioneer is someone who fights a tough battle on behalf of an entire industry, then Elon Musk definitely fits the description. For much of 2014, his Tesla Motors publicly fought with multiple states for the right to sell their cars directly to consumers without going through franchised dealerships, as all other automakers do.

Despite the long-standing battle, though, there are signs that Tesla's early arguments may be shifting the entire industry toward a more direct sales model ,and perhaps toward other business models as well. In 2014, automakers like Volvo and GM tested online car sales where buyers could negotiate all the elements of a car purchase online before working with a dealership only on the final step.

BMW has moved beyond car sales to offer a rental option for its electric cars through the BMW Drive Now program, which is piloting in selected cities across the United States, Germany and a handful of other countries.

Each of these pilot programs is shifting the traditional model for car sales to integrate more collaboration, fewer middleman relationships and more one-to-one experiences.

Delivering Value in Russia

When Russian e-retailer Lamoda decided to start selling fashion to customers across the country online, they ran into a big problem: the postal service in Russia was notoriously unreliable.

Rather than letting that steer the brand towards opening retail locations like others had done, they took surprising step of building their own fleet of hundreds of delivery vehicles and more than 700 couriers. These trained courier-advisors not only deliver products, but also stand by while customers try them on, decide what to keep, and even offer fashion advice.

This direct approach to retail has certainly been costly.

It is not easy to build your own infrastructure from the ground up to deliver products to a country as large as Russia. Yet the site is one of the fastest growing retailers in the sector, their delivery vehicles are increasingly familiar as Russians encounter them on the roads, and they already have more than 1.5 million customers and an estimated $240 million in revenue.

In 2014, thanks to its innovations in the supply chain model the retailer even attracted a €10 million financing from the IFC, a member of the World Bank Group and one of the largest global development institutions. The investment was centered on helping to support the regional development of the company's express delivery network, Lamoda Express, as a more modernized supply chain that could promote greater consumer spending.

Why It Matters

The pace of change in the music industry happens to be the perfect testing ground for a more direct model that many other industries are considering at the same time. Through the flux in music, automotive sales, retailing, academic journals and even the growth of a popular Russian e-retailer, the theme that emerges is that there is significant innovation coming not only in how products and services are made, but also in the way that they are distributed and sold. Most of that is focused on disrupting the traditional models of distributions that have sometimes been in place for decades.

It is this second element that has become far more important to track as a trend because it could potentially affect so many other types of businesses that are unrelated to any of these industries mentioned above.

Who Should Use This Trend?

Any business that sells products or services in a marketplace or through channels controlled by a central distributor will see some impact of this trend. The opportunity exists then, to find ways to leverage the audience you already have and deliver directly to those who want to buy from you.

In a world where the method for how you have sold your products or services and distributed them is undergoing seismic changes, how can you make sure your business is ready to survive? That is the ultimate question that this trend will force many businesses to confront in 2015.

How to Use This Trend

✓ **Make a big statement** – When a group of North Dakota farmers decided to create a restaurant on the East Coast called Founding Farmers, part of the idea was to bring the direct model of farm-to-table restaurants to Washington, DC. The aim, aside from reconnecting people to the growers and sources of their food, was to put a themed restaurant in a high-profile location filled with foodies and influential politicians. The lesson is an important one for leveraging the value of *Disruptive Distribution*: sometimes the ideal way to start is by creating a small pilot and building from that.

✓ **Take the better deal (even if it's not perfect)** – While the model of Lamoda is tempting, it is also hugely expensive and complex. The far easier path is to find a distribution model that is disruptive enough to offer *more* control. Amazon's model for book selling is a perfect example. It offers higher margins back to authors and publishers, yet it is still far from perfect because it also separates authors from readers while Amazon retains ownership of customer data. The point is, sometimes using *Disruptive Distribution* means taking the better option and getting as *close* to direct distribution as possible.

Chapter 18

MICROCONSUMPTION

·—·

What's the Trend?

As new payment models and products and experiences become available in bite-sized portions, multiple industries will experiment with micro-sized new forms of pricing and payments.

In 2014 one of the fastest growing social networks among young people under the age of 30 was built on a premise of allowing people to share a description for an activity that was once kept private: spending money.

Four years earlier, this surprisingly popular tool was first imagined by college friends and Venmo co-founders Andrew Kortina and Iqram Magdon-Ismail after one of them forgot his wallet on a trip to Philadelphia to visit the other. After borrowing $200 for that week, and struggling with the messy process of writing and depositing checks to settle up afterwards, the friends conceived an app as a solution to the problem.

At the time when the pair launched Venmo in 2010, plenty of competitive products existed, but none imagined that the process of sending payments might be an opportunity for *social engagement* as well.

This engagement was what made Venmo different from other mobile payment services. Users would send instant payments (linked directly to their bank accounts) and could also choose to share short Twitter-style payment summaries along with each payment.

These payment summaries were a chance for creativity and personality. Each short summary offered "a startlingly intimate look at people's social lives," as *Atlantic* writer Eric Levenson described. One user interviewed by Levenson took it even further, raving about how "it really does say so much about the little details of people's lives … I love all of it. I'm so nosy. It lets me be so nosy."

It seems plenty of users agree. In the first quarter of 2014, the Venmo app enabled $314 million in payments, which equaled the transaction volume of Starbucks' mobile payments app in the same time period.

What makes a simple mobile payment app that lets you share quick descriptions of how you are spending your money so appealing?

According to Magdon-Ismail, "one of the reasons people prefer us, and will prefer us in the future, is just the fact that we are social. You get more value out of sharing with friends."

There is a broader shift this represents. As friends get more used to talking about money, describing spending behavior and paying one another, they are also more easily sharing payments and expenses for everything from cab fares to bar tabs.

Ride sharing services like Uber and Lyft, for example, both offer fare-splitting features to allow friends to pay their own portions of the cab fare. A growing number of services and apps in multiple industries are seeking to apply the same principle to simplify shared payments.

Together, the rise of Venmo and fare splitting are examples of a broader shift that is affecting both how consumers expect to pay and how businesses are increasingly rethinking how they charge for them in the first place. This is *Microconsumption*.

Across the past year, one of most extreme shifts illustrated by this trend comes from how all kinds of experiences are now being priced and paid for.

Pay-Per-Laugh

At the Teatreneu in Barcelona, Spain, you won't get a money-back guarantee on the stand-up comedy shows they often feature. Instead, they make a simple promise: if the show isn't funny, you don't pay for it. Of course, you might be wondering how exactly they will know whether you think the show is funny. What if you're lying?

At Teatreneu, that would be impossible thanks to an innovative new payment model the theater launched to worldwide media attention last year. At Teatreneu, you pay per laugh.

The theater is the first to experiment with using facial recognition in all their theater seats to track exactly how often anyone laughs. The entrance to their shows is completely free, but show-goers link their credit cards to the tablets integrated into the back of each seat in the theater. Then throughout the show, the facial recognition technology will ideally detect every laugh and charge people 0.30 euros per laugh up to a maximum of 24 euros per show.

This "pay-per-laugh" model is the ultimate in micropayments, designed with extreme efficiency to make consumers feel better about only paying for real results.

The good news is this model also happens to be stunningly effective at generating revenue as well. Consumers generally pay a higher price, are happier with the experience, and Teatreneu reports that early results show a 35 percent increase in the number of attendees and an average of a 6 euro increase per ticket prices.

Screen-Sized Payments

DreamWorks Animation CEO Jeffrey Katzenberg has an intriguing prediction for the future of film based on a very simply financial reality: 98% of theatrical releases make 95% of their revenue within the first three weekends after release. After that, Katzenberg predicts distribution will shift to an immediate access payment model based on a "pay by the inch you watch" model.

He shared his views on the future of distributing and charging for films at Milken Global Conference in Beverly Hills in April 2014:

I think the model will change and you won't pay for the window of availability. A movie will come out and you will have 17 days, that's exactly three weekends, which is 95% of the revenue for 98% of *movies. On the 18th day, these movies will be available everywhere ubiquitously and you will pay for the size. A movie screen will be $15. A 75" TV will be $4.00. A smartphone will be $1.99. That enterprise that will exist throughout the world, when that happens, and it will happen, it will reinvent the enterprise of movies.*

This shift to pay-by-screen-size certainly fits the growing consumer usage of multiple devices for different moments in time. If consumers, as Katzenberg predicts, could be willing to pay different amounts for different screens—it is natural to think they may also choose *how* they consume content based on this pricing as well.

Wanted: Your Attention

As media consumption behavior continues to shift among consumers, advertisers are trying their best not to be far behind. This is a fact that the *Financial Times* newspaper's marketing and development director Jon Slade is counting on.

In 2014, the international media property was one of the first to talk about using "attention metrics" as a way to charge advertisers not by impressions or clicks, but rather by the amount of time that a consumer spent reading or interacting with a particular piece of content.

There is still plenty of debate as to whether this increased time on a particular page may help an advertiser at all in a world where more and more consumers have "banner blindness," where they ignore all advertising presented online.

Still, the combination of media properties reimagining how to charge advertisers for display ads, and the shift in how film studios might price new releases based on screen size point to the potential for new models of micropayment to change how many industries will charge for products and experiences in the future.

Why It Matters

As consumption moves to bite-sized content (as discussed extensively in the earlier chapter on *Glanceable Content*), a growing range of industries is experimenting with new ways to structure pricing for their experiences to match this behavior. Thanks to platforms like Venmo, consumers become used to small transactions and instant mobile-enabled payments. Beyond just allowing for micropayments, though, this trend illustrates that larger experiences too can be charged for in smaller pieces—even down to individual laughs at a comedy show.

As more consumption takes place in short bursts, and experiences can be charged for in tinier increments, this trend of *Microconsumption* will extend to more unexpected industries in 2015 as they also reimagine how they offer transactions or experiences.

Who Should Be Using This Trend?

The first to utilize this trend will be those in the content and media industries as they work to build new models for allowing people to pay for access, or to charge advertisers to reach those users. Outside of publishers of content, this trend will also be very important to watch for any organization that can find unique ways to break up its products or experiences into smaller pieces to enable more turnkey payments, particularly in a recurring fashion. Automotive manufacturers and car rental agencies will allow consumers to rent by the minute. Media sites will charge by the story. Any industry that can rethink how their current products and services are packaged and paid for can start to utilize this trend to prepare their own models for new opportunities in 2015.

How to Use This Trend

✓ **Be first to accept different payments** – The year 2014 was filled with announcements from a number of companies wanting to become the "first to accept bitcoin" in their industries. Air Baltic was the first airline. Meltdown Comics was the first comic book store. Time Inc. was the first major magazine publisher. In 2015, more brands will aim to be first at accepting new forms of payment. As they become easier to implement without big technology investments, this opportunity to be first will continue.

✓ **Produce more bite-sized content** – Related to the idea of making your content instantly glanceable, there is also a corresponding value to keep it short and consumable. When Netflix analyzed customer sessions, they realized that 87 percent of all mobile sessions lasted less than ten minutes. The only problem was, Netflix didn't have any content shorter than ten minutes long. As a result, the brand announced in 2014 its intentions to create 2–5 minute clips designed for mobile users. This same technique can help you target consumers' desire for *Microconsumption* as well, by giving them value in short, digestible bursts.

PART III

THE TREND
ACTION GUIDE

INTERSECTION THINKING:
How to Apply Trends to Your Business

"DISCOVERY CONSISTS OF SEEING WHAT EVERYBODY HAS
SEEN AND THINKING WHAT NOBODY HAS THOUGHT"
—ALBERT SZENT-GYÖRGYI, Nobel Prize–winning physician

In 2009 Tom Maas, a former marketing executive for distiller Jim Beam, finally created his perfect drink. For years he had been working on developing and promoting a new cream liquor based on the popular traditional milky cinnamon and almond drink from Latin America known as *horchata*.

This new drink, RumChata (a mashup of its primary liquor and the drink that inspired its flavors), was a mixture of light rum, dairy cream and spices like cinnamon and vanilla.

RumChata was not an instant hit.

The drink took some inventive selling, but when bartenders started comparing its taste to the milk at the bottom of a bowl of Cinnamon Toast Crunch cereal, it started to take off.

Bartenders started using the liquor to create more inspired blends, which quickly led to more liquor distributors and retailers carrying the brand. Meanwhile the brand ran inventive promotions like "cereal shooter bowls" designed for bars to serve RumChata based drinks and to further build the brand.

All the creativity finally started working.

A recent *BusinessWeek* article noted that the drink has taken one-fifth of the market share in the $1 billion U.S. market for cream-based liquors, and even started outselling Diageo's Baileys Irish Cream (the longstanding leader) in certain regions.

More importantly, experts described the drink as a game changer, due to its popularity as a mixer and its popularity as an ingredient for food and baking recipes.

How to Create a Game-Changing Product

RumChata is a perfect example of the type of result that can ultimately come from putting the power of observation together with an understanding for the intersection of consumer behavior and the open space in a market.

While Maas may not have used this same trend curation approach in order to come up with his product idea, we can still reverse engineer its success in order to find some lessons in the example.

When you do that, it becomes easy to spot a few of the big trends over the past several years that clearly support the concept of RumChata and perhaps explain some of its success:

- A growing consumer desire for authentic products with interesting backstories
- The rising prevalence of food entertainment programming on television inspiring more creativity in home cooking
- The increased interest across the United States in Hispanic culture and heritage

In retrospect, these observations clearly seem to support the arrival of a product like RumChata. Of course, putting the dots together looking backwards is easy.

The real question is: how can you do it predictably in a way that can help you to create your own success in the near future?

An Introduction to Intersection Thinking

Trends are typically big ideas describing the accelerating world around us. Unfortunately, the value of big ideas are not always easily understood when it comes to applying them to real life situations.

Trend forecaster Chris Sanderson from *The Future Laboratory* describes trends as "profits waiting to happen." As tempting as that sounds, realizing those profits takes more than skill at uncovering, curating and describing a trend.

Trends only have value if you can learn to apply them.

Is a trend telling you to abandon an existing product line? Or to pivot the focus of your business? Or to stay the course in a direction that hasn't yet paid off? These are the sorts of big questions that each of us is likely to contend with in our own business and career, and they are not easy to answer.

The good news is that we can usually find the answers if we apply the right model of thinking. The rest of this section is dedicated to giving you the tools, processes and knowledge to be able to apply trends in your own business and career.

Over the past several years of helping organizations and students learn to apply trends, my approach always starts with the single simple concept of intersection.

Intersection thinking is a method for creating overlap between seemingly disconnected ideas in order to generate new ideas, directions and strategies for powering your own success.

Most of the time, I have used a workshop model to help teams and brands apply intersection thinking to their own challenges in order to create new approaches based on trends in the marketplace. The chapters following this one offer a step –by-step approach to take you through four of the most popular workshop models I typically use. Before engaging in these workshops, it is useful to share three basic principles behind applying intersection thinking in real life.

PRINCIPLE #1: SEE THE SIMILARITIES INSTEAD OF THE DIFFERENCES.

Paolo Nagari is an intercultural intelligence expert who teaches executives the skills they need to succeed while living overseas. Unlike many other experts, however, his model doesn't rely on teaching the "dos and don'ts" of a particular culture. Succeeding in a culture other than your own takes more than book knowledge.

Nagari's first rule for executives is all about learning to focus on the many similarities in cultures instead of the differences. It is a valuable lesson when considering how to apply unfamiliar trends as well.

Though the stories or industry behind a certain trend may seem disconnected from your own, there are always more similarities than you think. When former Coca-Cola executive Jeff Dunn became president of Bolthouse Farms in 2008, for example, he walked into a billion-dollar agricultural company that had literally reinvented the carrot industry by creating "baby carrots."

By the time Dunn took over, sales of carrots (and baby carrots) were experiencing a slump and he needed a solution, so he turned to advertising agency Crispin Porter + Bogusky (CP+B).

It wasn't the usual challenge for the agency, but they offered a unique idea for a solution based on a single insight: people love snacking on junk food and hate being told to eat healthier.

As CP+B creative director Omid Farhang later told *Fast Company* "the truth about baby carrots is they possess many of the defining characteristics of our favorite junk food. They're neon orange, they're crunchy, they're dippable, they're kind of addictive."

Using this insight, CP+B built a new campaign that enticed consumers to "Eat 'Em Like Junk Food," inspired by the marketing tactics of other consumer packaged goods companies (like Coca-Cola). In campaign test markets, sales were up between 10% and 12%, all thanks to a campaign built from seeing the similarities between the wildly divergent products of junk food and vegetables.

PRINCIPLE #2: PURPOSELY LOOK AWAY FROM YOUR GOAL.

Frans Johansson is a keen observer of people and companies. His first book, *The Medici Effect*, talked beautifully about the power of intersections between diverse industries and people as a way of generating game-changing ideas, products and organizations.

In his second book, *The Click Moment*, he focuses on the related idea of serendipity in our lives and what any of us might do in order to increase the chances of having our own serendipitous meetings or interactions with others.

In this second book he also retells the well-known origin story of the inspiration behind Starbucks, found on a trip Howard Schultz took to Milan, where he saw the dominance of the Italian espresso coffee shops on every street corner and imagined that a similar type of establishment might work in America as well.

His insight led to a pivot for Starbucks from a supplier of high-end home brewing equipment to a retail coffee establishment. The original purpose of his trip to Milan was only to attend a trade show.

It was only on a chance walk from his hotel to the convention center that he noticed and became inspired by these espresso bars. His story illustrates that sometimes it is better to explore ideas outside your main goal so you can see even bigger ideas waiting to be discovered.

PRINCIPLE 3: WANDER INTO THE UNFAMILIAR.

If you happen to be walking the streets of Bangkok around 6pm on any particular day, you will see people stop in their tracks for seemingly inexplicable reasons. Ask anyone afterwards and you will quickly learn that there are two times every day when the Thai national anthem is played (8am and 6pm) and all citizens stop what they are doing and observe a moment of silence out of respect.

Once you see this cultural choice in practice, it is impossible to forget.

Travel experiences are like this—whether they happen across the world from your home, or simply during a visit to an unfamiliar place. Wandering is a form of exploration that we often think to embrace only when traveling, but it has great value on a more daily basis.

In a world where we have a map in our pocket, ready to assist us with turn-by-turn directions to anywhere, wandering must be a choice. It is the perfect metaphor for why intersection thinking matters, and why it can be difficult as well.

Now that I have shared three principles for using intersection thinking, let's talk about how to apply trends to your own situation with the tool I use most frequently—*workshops*.

Why Workshops Work

A workshop is a defined moment in time where an individual or a group of people can focus on discussing a particular concept and generating powerful ideas on how to use that it effectively.

While it may seem like a complicated endeavor (particularly if you are looking to apply trends more individually for yourself and your own career), there are several reasons to consider taking a workshop-driven approach to applying trends.

1. **Focus your attention.** We are busy and usually don't have the time to be sitting around thinking about trends all day. To ensure you can have the right focused attention, I always recommend blocking out a set period of time for a workshop, even if it happens to be minimal. Just the act of making sure this time is scheduled and separate from your usual daily activities will help ensure that it feels and actually becomes significant.

2. **Follow a defined process.** There are many ways to engineer the structure of what you do in a workshop. I will share several of them in later chapters to help you get started. Whichever you choose, the important thing is that, like any good meeting, your workshop has the right structure so participants know what you aim to accomplish and can commit to the same shared goals.

3. **Establish accountability.** Another critical reason that workshops can be so effective is that they help bring the right people together in a single moment so they can make commitments about action steps and what to do next. Accountability, of course, is equally important if you happen to be working alone to decide how to apply these trends.

Almost every one of the dozens of workshops I have given on marketing and business trends and the future starts the same way, with a presentation of the trends. Yet it is important to remember that most of the time, *the ultimate goal is not to uncover new trends.*

A workshop is most useful after you have *already* used the process in the first part of the book to curate your own trends, or selected trends produced by others (such as those featured in Part II of this book). The goal of any trend workshop is to take those trends and discuss how to put them into action to solve your business challenges.

5 Keys to Running a Great Trend Workshop

When considering using a workshop, there are a few basic ground rules to keep in mind to help you get the best result:

1. **Always have an unbiased facilitator** – It is easy to assume that the person closest to the issue will be the right person to lead a workshop, but this is often not true. Instead, the best workshop leaders are individuals who can lead a discussion, keep a conversation on track and ask bold questions without being biased or intentionally leading a group toward a particular answer or point of view.

2. **Encourage sharing, not critiquing** – We have all heard the common cliché that there are "no bad ideas in a brainstorm." That's not technically true. There *are* bad ideas, off-strategy ideas, impossible ideas and useless ideas. Unfortunately, they are rarely easy to distinguish in the real time environment of a workshop. For that reason, the best mentality to encourage for all participants is one where everyone commits to sharing new ideas that can be captured rather than wasting time and energy trying to critique an idea.

3. **Adopt a "yes and" mindset** – Stand up comedians always talk about the importance of following a scene and adding to the narrative by always saying "yes and" instead of "yes but" (its far more negative cousin). This additive approach allows you to build upon what others have shared instead of breaking it down, and it is one of the consistent hallmarks of great and effective workshops.

4. **Prepare like a pro** – If you have ever heard the phrase "garbage in, garbage out"—you should know this applies tenfold to workshops. If you have not prepared the right materials, insights and questions before a workshop, you will rarely be able to generate great value. This doesn't mean spending months on research, but you should have the right background to make sure all the participants are informed enough to offer value back during the workshop.

5. **Recap and summarize** – One of the worst things to do after committing the time and expense to running a workshop is to let everyone in the room leave without summarizing what took place over the time you shared together. It is the role of the facilitator to summarize the conversation, recap any action items and ensure that everyone who spent their precious time participating understands what they collectively achieved and what will need to happen next in order to keep the momentum going.

The Four Models of Trend Workshops

While the formats and methods you might use in this type of workshop setting are almost endless, the next several chapters in this section will take you through four specific models for how to apply trends strategically based on differing goals.

Here are the four formats we will cover in the following chapters.

- **Customer Journey Mapping Trend Workshop** – Building a step-by-step understanding of how your customers interact with you so you can apply trends to each step of the process.
- **Brand Storytelling Trend Workshop** – Developing a powerful brand story or message designed to resonate with customers based on understanding and using current trends.
- **Business Strategy Trend Workshop** – Creating a new go-to-market or product-launch strategy or making changes to a business model or revenue model informed by current trends.

- **Company Culture Trend Workshop** – Planning your career or optimizing an internal company culture and team based on current trends.

For Small Teams

A final consideration I will share before digging into each of these workshops is how to apply them if you happen to be a sole proprietor or owner of a very small company without a large team of people to participate in something like a workshop.

Although the following chapters are specifically written from the point of view of having multiple participants in each type of workshop, many of the lessons in these chapters can be easily applied to small businesses individually as well.

It may be tempting to dismiss the value of workshops or even intersection thinking if you happen to be on your own, but I encourage you to give these approaches a chance. Just because you don't have an army of team members doesn't mean you can't use the benefits of intersection thinking and workshops to power your business as well.

HOW TO USE A CUSTOMER JOURNEY
MAPPING TREND WORKSHOP

"GREAT BRANDS ARE MEANT TO BE GREAT
AGGREGATORS. WE'RE MEANT TO BE THE
ONES THAT ARE OUT THERE LISTENING TO
WHAT'S HAPPENING IN THE WORLD ...
AND AGGREGATING IT.
—KEVIN PLANK, CEO of Under Armour

Visionary leaders have the ability to get inside a consumer's mind.

They understand what people want, sometimes even before the consumers themselves realize it. Yet intuition is a hard thing to quantify, and an even harder thing to duplicate. Mapping a customer journey step by step is a process anyone can follow whether they happen to have a finely tuned intuition for consumer needs or not.

In this chapter, you will learn how to combine a map of your customer's journey with a knowledge of important trends to inform how you might change the way you reach that customer. Ultimately, the aim is to offer them a better solution, capture their attention more easily, and stand out among your competitors.

What Is Customer Journey Mapping?

A customer journey map is a diagram that illustrates the progression your ideal customer goes through when interacting with your brand, from consideration to purchase and loyalty.

If this progression sounds familiar, it is because most business or marketing courses in school teach this same model, calling it the "purchase funnel" or the "buying cycle." No matter what you call it, the *phases* of a customer journey will typically come down to the following six distinct moments for any brand or product:

THE SIX PHASES OF A CUSTOMER JOURNEY

PHASE 0 – Customer doesn't know they need the product or service
What to call this phase: pre-awareness, pre-service, need generation

PHASE 1 – Customer has a need and starts seeking potential solutions
What to call this phase: awareness, consideration, researching

PHASE 2 – Customer finds solutions and starts comparing alternatives
What to call this phase: consideration, comparison, shopping, evaluation

PHASE 3 – Customer buys product, receives it and initially uses it
What to call this phase: purchase, buying, conversion, delivery, installation

PHASE 4 – Customer uses and experiences the product
What to call this phase: usage, engagement, experience, activation

PHASE 5 – Customer talks about product to others or considers repurchasing
What to call this phase: advocacy, loyalty, retention, sharing, recommendation

---

Depending on your product or service, this model may immediately seem too complex. Usually, if some of these phases seem as though they don't exist for your situation, it may only be because they happen so fast that it seems you can't influence them.

When a customer buys a Snickers bar, for example, the idea that they are comparing alternatives may seem like over-analysis. How much consideration really goes into an impulse buy? Yet, even in that split-second decision at a checkout aisle, a customer is still going through the progression of their customer journey and thinking about each phase.

OBJECTIVE:
When Should You Use This Workshop?

The customer journey mapping workshop is ideal for helping you to define specific tactics that you can implement in various parts of your business immediately to reach consumers at the most opportune times in their buying process. While other workshops can help you focus more on business strategy or overall brand messaging, this one is focused on small changes to implement quickly in order to impact how you sell and deliver experiences to your customers.

PREPARATION:
What to Do Before the Workshop

Prior to this workshop, it is important to have a well-defined idea of not only who your customers are, but the journey they currently use.

Building out a customer journey map can sometimes be the result of real field research with consumers. Other times, it is developed with a separate workshop model intended to help illuminate the entire journey that your customers typically go through.

In particular, here are a few elements that have value to develop prior to running a trend workshop on customer journey mapping:

1. **Customer Journey Maps** – The visual customer journey map is a valuable asset to have as you work to understand your customer(s). The aim of the customer journey mapping trend

workshop is not to develop this map in the workshop but rather to use it as a blueprint upon which to add strategies and tactics for using trends. For that reason, this is perhaps the most important element of preparation to develop before the workshop. In case you need help to do it or have never completed one of these, see later in this chapter for a list of resources to help you get started.

2. **Personas** – Personas allow you to create a model for a typical customer that is more human and descriptive so it helps the entire team to picture *someone* rather than a segment of people or a demographic when considering tactics. Often these personas are written in narrative format, and a corresponding visual image of the customer to make it even more real. Personas are most often built from existing customer research or from a customer already profiled or interviewed.

3. **Stakeholder Maps** – A stakeholder map lets you consider audiences outside of customers, such as board members, the media and partners. The idea of visualizing or listing out those stakeholders allows you to have a filter from which to consider new ideas and ensure they are aimed at the right people.

4. **Customer Segments** – Most businesses rarely have a single type of customer at all times. Instead, they have multiple segments based on product lines, regional considerations or even various times of year. Knowing these segments can also help you to define that customer journey and to see how much it might vary from segment to segment. Many times, a similar approach can work across segments. Sometimes, you may need to divide a workshop to treat segments completely separately.

PARTICIPANTS:
Who Should Be Involved in the Workshop?

There is no set rule about who needs to be involved in a particular workshop, but even if you are working in a small business with only yourself or one other person, using a workshop model may still have great value for you.

The list below is based on the ideal number of participants for this workshop, if you can manage to get the right people involved and have a large enough team or extended circle of participants:

1. **Facilitator (1)** – The facilitator is the leader of the conversation and is responsible primarily for keeping the session on track, posing big questions, probing further when needed, ensuring no single participant dominates and summarizing the session and some of the discussion's big takeaways.

2. **Scribe (1)** – The point of having the task of recording notes separated from the facilitator role is so the facilitator is free to focus on the conversation. The scribe, however, must do more than simply record what is said. He or she needs to be able to apply enough insight to capture the essence of ideas and connect them in real time.

3. **Participants (2–12)** – Taking on a fairly straightforward role, these are the people who will be part of the workshop and deliver ideas and value. The ideal number of participants ranges from 6–12 for most of these workshops I have run in the past, but it is heavily dependent on the preferences of the facilitator and the people in the room.

4. **Voice of the Customer (1)** – It is important to try and involve someone who is closer to the customers and their journey, and who can represent the voice of the customer in the room at all times. This person may also play another role as well, but it is important to nominate *someone* to be the customer's advocate during the workshop because they can also offer a mindset that is easy to forget.

5. **Graphic Facilitator (Optional)** – One of my favorite additions to this workshop, because it is so visual, is a graphic facilitator to capture the conversation through illustrations

on a large board in real time. While this is typically offered by a third-party group and may require some extra budget, the value of doing this can be transformative in how much impact the workshop can have beyond the immediate participants.

FORMAT:
How Should the Workshop Be Structured?

Rather than recommend one model for every situation, I am including the descriptions of three common models that I have used in different situations based on the people in the room to help map out how trends can affect your customer journey.

You can select one of these methods, or develop your own style for how to structure the conversation. Any one can work, as long as you are building the right type of experience tailored to bring out the best in the participants you are working with.

1. **"Day In The Life" Customer Journey Mapping Trend Workshop** – This model focuses on taking a step-by-step approach to reaching a customer at various points throughout his or her day. Based on the customer persona, the participants can build a schedule of a consumer's average day. Then, the ideation can focus on how trends shape each customer's day differently and what that means for changing how the brand currently interacts with the customer in those moments.

2. **"Customer Of The Future" Customer Journey Mapping Trend Workshop** – The discussion in this workshop focuses on contrasting your customers' existing journey against the how it may be changing due to the trends you have uncovered. The aim is to develop ways to better reach and influence these customers in the midst of this change.

3. **"Early Adopter" Customer Journey Mapping Trend Workshop** – This workshop is built on the premise of spotlighting and applying lessons from your earliest customers and

looking at them in the context of trends to create a model for what to do first and whom to target.

RESULTS:
What Is the Benefit of the Workshop?

In a customer journey mapping trend workshop, the ultimate aim is to apply trends to change the way that you interact with customers or understand their needs and desires. Beyond shaping an overall strategy, this workshop is also likely to generate many ideas for how to change small aspects of your customer experience to leverage trend insights and be ready for the changing world of consumers.

CASE STUDY: Imagine You Own
a Local Hiking & Outdoor Activities Store

Like most others, you have challenges to your business coming from larger competitors and the growing ranks of consumers who turn to the web for one-click ordering of just about anything.

How do you compete?

This workshop could help you develop a strategy to do that. Assuming you don't already have one, the first thing you would do is develop a map of your customer's usual journey by either asking a targeted series of questions either directly to consumers or developing a list and then answering it based on observing how they behave.

Here are a few example questions you might ask:

- Do they have a trip planned before they come to your store with specific needs or do they simply browse before booking a trip?
- If they have a trip planned, how soon are they typically leaving, within a day or a week or a month?
- Do they come for expert advice and then go off and seek a better price offline or follow expert advice and buy immediately?

- What situations are they commonly in where it might be appropriate for them to talk about your store with others?

You can immediately see how these sorts of questions give you a strong sense of their journey, and you can use the resources shared at the end of this chapter to map out this customer journey if you haven't already.

From there, you can start to apply your knowledge of consumer and business trends to this journey to build a plan of action to better compete in the coming year. Here are a few examples of how to start to map the trends to the insights you already have about your customers:

1. **How to Use *Everyday Stardom*** – Just as some Thai restaurants feature a "wall of flame" for those few customers who finished a bowl of curry with a spice level of 10, you might offer something similar to create an emotional reason for customers to continually come back and see you during the *usage phase* (Phase 4).

2. **How to Use *Reverse Retail*** – How robust is your online store when it comes to giving consumers an online alternative rather than simply price checking Amazon when they are in the *buying phase* (Phase 3)? Making it easy and directing them online can be the best of both worlds, highly convenient for them, and allowing you to keep less inventory in store.

3. **How to Use *Mass Mindfulness*** – What if instead you could offer a compelling experience that appeals to your customers' view of the world? If your customers love the outdoors, could you offer a class or new product demo as a way to connect and offer more value for them? Doing this proactively can help you reach potential customers during their *consideration phase* (Phase 1) or even in that phase when they haven't yet decided to buy anything and are *not looking* (Phase 0).

These three trends were selected randomly and I used them to illustrate how trends can be applied directly to a business. Depending on your industry, you may not need every trend, or you may use trends that you have uncovered in your own research rather than those in this book.

Either way, using your customer's journey as a starting point can help you to generate your own valuable ideas for how to apply these trends to better promote your business or share your message with the world.

RESOURCES: Where Can I Learn More about Customer Journeys?

I recommend the following valuable resources to those seeking to learn more about Customer Journey Mapping. You can also share them with a broader team to help everyone achieve alignment before hosting a workshop:

1. **Smaply (www.smaply.com)** – Perhaps the most complete software available online to be able to easily create customer journey maps and a number of other resources discussed in this section like stakeholder maps and personas. Highly recommended.

2. *Unfolding the Napkin* **by Dan Roam** – Learning to visualize a problem is a particularly important skill for customer journey mapping and this workshop, and Roam's book is a favorite resource I often recommend to my students in order to help them learn the art of visual thinking and drawing.

3. *Smashing Magazine* **(www.smashingmagazine.com)** – Though created as a website primarily for web designers and developers, *Smashing Magazine* has a wealth of content on creating customer journey maps as well as visual thinking and just about anything else relating to creating powerful design and digital efforts. When it comes to design resources to help you think better, this one is at the top of the list.

For an online list featuring these resources and many more, please visit the link below:

WWW.ROHITBHARGAVA.COM/NONOBVIOUS/RESOURCES

HOW TO USE A BRAND STORYTELLING TREND WORKSHOP

"WHEN YOU WANT TO MOVE SOMEBODY, YOU HAVE TO SAY TO YOURSELF: 'I'M IN THE EMOTIONAL TRANSPORTATION BUSINESS. I GOTTA MOVE THEM, EMOTIONALLY.'"

—PETER GUBER, Hollywood producer
and best-selling author of *Tell To Win*

A powerful story is a reason to believe in your brand and products—and it always matters.

Trends can also have a big impact on how you tell your brand story. For example, in Chapter 7, I focused on the trend of *Branded Benevolence* and how it also describes the increasing importance consumers are placing on the ethical practices of brands. These are examples of the elements of a brand's story and they are critical to inspire more loyalty and consideration among consumers.

This chapter will explore some models for hosting a brand storytelling workshop that takes the lessons from recent trends and applies them to how you can tell a stronger and more emotional story for your business.

Sometimes, this may mean adding an element to an existing story you already use for your brand. Other times, it may require you tell an entirely new story influenced by the trends. Either way, the techniques in this chapter will help.

Why Does Brand Storytelling Matter?

Brand storytelling means sharing the story of your brand in an emotional way in order to inspire belief and increase engagement with your customers.

There is a growing body of evidence that shows just how powerful and necessary these stories happen to be.

To illustrate why stories matter, consider the example of Significant Objects, a website two writers named Joshua Glenn and Rob Walker created in 2012. As an experiment, the creators asked a hundred noted authors to craft stories for products purchased at a garage sale for an average of $1.29 each.

The resulting stories helped them sell the corresponding objects on eBay for more than $8000 dollars, illustrating how much difference a story makes in how much people are willing to pay for a product.

Unfortunately, all this attention on the necessity of storytelling for marketing and promoting a brand doesn't always lead us towards *good* stories. The web is filled with boring "About Us" pages that share little more than a timeline of activities, mergers, office moves and notable hires. None of these is the same as a story.

Unfortunately, if you don't have a well-described brand story behind your mission and your products *already*, running a workshop to update or inform your brand story won't help you.

In my first book, *Personality Not Included*, I featured a model for learning how to develop and share your brand story inspired by techniques from Hollywood screenwriters and filmmakers. If you need to start with developing or updating your own brand story first, see the end of this chapter for a link to a page of resources that includes several free excerpts and downloads from that book to help you.

You may choose to use one of the five models I present in *Personality Not Included*, or develop your own story independently. Either way, it is important to be sure that you have a well-constructed brand story *before* you start with using this particular workshop to improve and inform it with current trends.

OBJECTIVE:
When Should You Use This Workshop?

Customer sentiments are always changing and no matter how powerful your brand story, there is always going to be a need to go back and make sure it is still as current and valuable as it could be. This workshop is ideal to consider using on an annual basis to review your existing brand story, the way it is shared and what could be optimized for the coming year based on the current trends.

Apart from annually, this can also be particularly valuable if you are in the midst of launching a new product series or shifting the focus of your business in some way that may require you to reconsider how you have previously been sharing the story of your business with the world.

PREPARATION:
What to Do Before the Workshop

The most important piece of preparation for this workshop (aside from *having* a brand story!) is to collect and audit the different channels and assets that exist to share your brand story. This includes everything from websites and landing pages, to brochures and reports, to packaging materials. Anything that supports your brand story could be relevant, and having an audit of all these materials is important so you can focus the scope of your workshop.

The other thing that can help you prepare for this workshop, depending on the structure you choose to use, is research on competitor messages and stories that are being used in the marketplace as well. The more you know about what stories your competitors are telling, the more you can work to build a strategy that stands out as being unique.

PARTICIPANTS:
Who Should Be Involved?

Like the customer journey mapping trend workshop, there is no set rule about who needs to be involved in a brand storytelling workshop. Once again, if you are working in a small business with only you or one other person, following this process can still offer some valuable outputs for you to consider.

The list below is a recommended starting point based on my previous experiences running this type of workshop:

1. **Facilitator (1)** – The facilitator is the leader of the conversation and is responsible primarily for keeping the session on track, posing big questions, probing further when needed, ensuring no single participant dominates and summarizing the session and some of the discussion's big takeaways.

2. **Scribe (1)** – The point of having the task of recording notes separated from the facilitator role is so the facilitator is free to focus on the conversation. The scribe, however, must do more than simply record what is said. He or she needs to be able to apply enough insight to capture the essence of ideas and connect them in real time.

3. **Participants (2–4)** – For a storytelling workshop, working with a smaller group is preferable because storytelling can be so subjective. The reality is that most of the time a core group of people will usually work on building out most of the storytelling on behalf of a brand anyway, so having the most important people in the room instead of every possible stakeholder is more efficient.

4. **Content Creators (1–2)** – Based on the results of this workshop, there will likely be some people who then need to go

and produce content in some form (written, audio or video). Having at least one of those creators involved in the workshop can have a lot of value in making sure the decisions and conversations aren't lost in translation. The other benefit is the content creator feels invested in the process and empowered to add value as well.

FORMAT:
How Should the Workshop Be Structured?

Brand storytelling workshops are often the most unique and creative, which makes them particularly interesting and exciting. Unfortunately, they can also hold the greatest potential for losing focus and turning into less valuable diversions. To ensure that your workshop stays on track, it is important to use a structured approach for exactly *how* the participants will be talking about storytelling.

The following two models share examples of approaches that have worked in the past for encouraging ideation and discussion without getting off track. When paired with a strong deliverable at the end of the workshop (particularly if working in teams to solve challenges) then these can be very effective:

1. **"Origin & Backstory" Brand Storytelling Trend Workshop** – Perhaps the most frequently read story behind most brands is the story of how the company or products first came together. What was the inspiration behind your brand? Does it connect with consumers in this modern media landscape? This workshop model tackles those questions by focusing the dialogue on the founder(s) and origin story of your brand, and then asks questions related to how the new trends might change or inform that story.

2. **"Customer As Hero" Brand Storytelling Trend Workshop** – Another way to think about the brand story is by painting a picture of your employee as the real hero and voice behind your brand. In this model, you work to use trends to inform how your story can be told from a customer's point of view

and how that might shift given the new consumer, culture and media trends identified in the market.

RESULTS:
What Is the Benefit of the Workshop?

The ultimate aim of this workshop is to optimize your brand story in a way that uses the latest trends to be more powerful, believable or effective. Doing that requires an understanding of how the story is currently being told and the touch points either in the story itself or in the channels you use to share it that can be adapted.

When done right, this workshop can help you bring your existing story into the future and deliver it in a way that maximizes how effective that story is likely to be.

CASE STUDY:
Imagine You Work at a Mid-Sized Law Firm

You work with individuals (B2C) and businesses (B2B) and have several different specialty practice areas. When it comes to communication, you are also dealing in a very serious and regulated area, where every piece of communication must be deliberate and there is little appetite for wild innovation or unproven experimentation.

How can you use trends to more authoritatively tell your story to the world without breaking industry conventions or being too informal?

The first step in storytelling is to break out of the feature-biased way that most of us think to describe ourselves. **A list of bullet points is not a story.**

Instead, think about why your clients trust in your brand and what they believe when they choose to work directly with you. Do they select you based on the reputation of your partners? Do they come based on personal recommendations? Do you have various client groups with wildly different reasons for doing anything?

Asking these sorts of questions can lead you toward thinking through how to apply specific trends to your brand story as you currently share it. For example, here are a few ways that *2015 Non-Obvious Trends* might transform how you share your brand story:

1. **How to Use *Glanceable Content*** – The shrinking human attention span is a truth to be faced in any industry, but in the world of professional services it also means that you need to deliver the story of your benefits and unique value more quickly and with less fanfare. This could mean rewriting headlines on print brochures or websites, but it also might lead to a shift in how legal documents themselves are prepared, and a company-wide focus on using more plain language.

2. **How to Use *Unperfection*** – No one likes to admit mistakes, and in the legal world this type of admission could lead to liability. Even so, using this trend to demonstrate the humanity of your colleagues and firm can help to inspire *more* trust instead of less. Consider, for example, if lawyers shared a bit of quirky personal information in their executive bios to add more of a human element. Prospective clients seeking representation by humans instead of legally trained robots (in other words, most people) can much better connect with real people. This approach may lead them to see your firm as being easier to work with and more desirable.

3. **How to Use *Branded Benevolence*** – Most firms have some type of philanthropy program, but any discussions of it is typically limited to how many hours were donated by employees or how much money was donated by the firm itself. Instead, why not encourage more everyday acts of kindness, such as small donations from employees to individual crowdfunding campaigns or applauding stories of employees' personal philanthropic efforts. These stories go much further than bullet points to illustrate the real principles your firm believes in and why you may be worth doing business with.

Every law firm, just like any brand, has an appetite for new innovation and different ideas. Yours may fall low or high on the spectrum of innovators. Regardless of how forward-thinking you consider your business to be, the trends are only a framework to allow you think about what you need to do or change next in how you currently operate.

The examples above are selected at random and applied to a very specific type of business (a mid-sized law firm), but the broader picture this example provides is just how flexible these trends can be to lead to changes in your brand story to help you inspire more belief and advocacy from your customer base.

RESOURCES: Where Can I Learn More about Brand Storytelling?

The following are several valuable resources to help you with developing or adapting your brand story:

1. *Resonate* by **Nancy Duarte** – This is one of my favorite resources to recommend when it comes to developing an amazing presentation to deliver on stage or build a more powerful brand story. Not only will this book help you develop graphics to visualize your story, it will also give you a proven blueprint for making any story as effective as possible.

2. *Tell to Win* by **Peter Guber** – Guber's book is filled with anecdotes and personal stories from his meetings with some of the most amazing storytellers in the world. This book will take you inside conversations with masters like David Copperfield and the Dalai Lama and distill those lessons into valuable nuggets of wisdom you can use in your own storytelling efforts.

3. *Lead with a Story* by **Paul Smith** – The research bias behind this book makes it a particularly valuable read to help you quantify and improve your ability to not only share stories with consumers, but also to use them for leadership and inspiration for your employees and the people closest to your brand who are in the position of sharing your story on your behalf.

For an online list featuring these resources and many more (including a free chapter on storytelling from *Personality Not Included*), please visit the link below:

WWW.ROHITBHARGAVA.COM/NONOBVIOUS/RESOURCES

HOW TO USE A BUSINESS STRATEGY TREND WORKSHOP

"HOWEVER BEAUTIFUL THE STRATEGY,
YOU SHOULD OCASSIONALLY LOOK AT THE RESULTS."
—WINSTON CHURCHILL, British prime minister

What if you had to change the way that you sell your products or services overnight?

The most powerful potential of using trends is that they can sometimes lead you to make a big shift in the strategy of your business itself, rather than just how you promote it. The inspiration for this workshop, therefore, comes from brands looking to evolve their business models and approaches to meet changing consumer demands.

In previous years, broader business trends around the collaborative economy or the rise of apps have enabled new ways to sell and buy. One of my 2014 trends described this shift in terms of *Subscription Commerce*, where brands in multiple industries from movie theaters to auto manufacturers started using subscriptions as new ways to sell products or experiences previously sold only a la carte.

In this chapter, we will look at the different elements of a business strategy and how you can start to think about applying trends to the strategy you use for running your business. Whether you have a well-scripted business strategy or the idea of a business strategy seems like overkill, this chapter should help you think about how the latest business trends might apply and be worth thinking about.

What Is Business Strategy?

Of course you already know what business strategy is, but my reason for posing the question here is to make sure we have a shared understanding of a few *components* of strategy that this workshop can help you to address.

Your business strategy is more than just a statement of what you sell.

Here are five specific elements of your strategy that doing this workshop may be helpful with:

1. **Mission** – Why you do what you do (and what you believe in).
2. **Positioning** – What makes your brand unique compared to your competitors.
3. **Business Model** – How you charge your customers and make money.
4. **Products and Services** – What you sell to your customers.
5. **Innovation for the Future** – Which new products or services you may offer later.

The rest of this chapter will share some techniques and methods to review these five elements and how they may be changing for your business when you think about the impact of trends on them.

OBJECTIVE:
When Should You Use This Workshop?

While there is no set timetable within which you need to review your business strategy, it may be a valuable thing to do on an annual basis simply because many trend reports and new research come out at the start of the year that could be worth considering.

Apart from that, here are a few other situations when it may make sense to review your overall business strategy:

- A new competitor is changing the landscape of your industry.
- There are new or different regional challenges to your business.
- Technological innovation has advanced the way your industry generally operates.
- Consumer expectation has shifted dramatically in your industry.
- You have a new innovative product or service to introduce to the market.
- Leadership at your organization has changed, and the new leader wants to make his or her mark.

There are likely many other situations where this workshop may be helpful, but this list includes some of the most common.

PREPARATION:
What to Do Before the Workshop?

Preparation for this workshop depends on the type of focus it will have, however the more information you can collect about the way you currently do business and how you make money, the better. It is also useful to collect any publicly available information about the mission of your organization and those used by your competitors.

Having any sort of visual or description of your business model as well as a map of all your products and services (both existing and planned) can also help in this workshop.

PARTICIPANTS:
Who Should Be Involved?

The roles for a workshop with this trend are fairly similar to those in earlier workshops. The key difference for a strategic workshop is that it tends to work better with fewer participants because a strategy session tends to accomplish more real decisions in the actual workshop as opposed to generating a framework for later work and implementation.

Given this recommendation, here is suggested list of participants:

1. **Facilitator (1)** – The facilitator is the leader of the conversation and is responsible primarily for keeping the session on track, posing big questions, probing further when needed, ensuring no single participant dominates and summarizing the session and some of the discussion's big takeaways.

2. **Scribe (1)** – The point of having the task of recording notes separated from the facilitator role is so the facilitator is free to focus on the conversation. The scribe, however, must do more than simply record what is said. He or she needs to be able to apply enough insight to capture the essence of ideas and connect them in real time.

3. **Participants (2–4)** – When discussing business strategy, working with a smaller group of participants is preferable because it is easier to reach a consensus and map out real decisions during the workshop. Ideal participants in this workshop may also include outside advisors, investors or others who may not be part of the day-to-day operations of a business but have a valuable point of view to share at a higher level.

FORMAT:
How Should the Workshop Be Structured?

The best business strategy trend workshops start with a clear idea of the challenge or issue you are working to solve. Articulating a good question to start your workshop will lead you toward better solutions and strategies coming out of the workshop. While the challenge you focus on could be almost anything, here are a few common challenges or business issues that might inspire you to hold a business strategy trend workshop:

- You are losing market share or sales for some reason (known or unknown).
- One of your competitors is growing rapidly and affecting your business.
- You have some resourcing challenge around hiring or retaining the best people.
- There has been some new regulation or industry change that creates a new opportunity.

Once you know your business challenge, you can focus the conversation during a workshop to think about how you can shift your business strategy to address it. To do this, there are two models for workshops I have typically used to help brands rethink their business strategy:

1. **"Model Recreation" Business Strategy Trend Workshop** – Every good trend has examples of brands and organizations that are using the trend well. These success stories can offer the perfect backdrop for a workshop discussion on how your own brand could apply exactly the same lessons. To use it, select a company (or several) that use a business strategy your team considers to be innovative. Use those brands as templates to think about how your company could try to do *exactly* what they do. Then, you can step back and discuss how to make it practical and build from this extreme vision to something more customized.

2. **"Tagline Roulette" Business Strategy Trend Workshop** – One of the most shocking things you can do to start any discussion about brand positioning is compare your company tagline with those from your competitors. Most of the time, it is hard to tell which is which. Building from this list of surprisingly generic taglines (as they usually are), challenge workshop participants to use trends to think differently about how to describe the unique value of your business with language that your competitors aren't using. This challenge often leads to reconsidering the business strategy behind it.

RESULTS:
What Is the Benefit of the Workshop?

The business strategy trend workshop is designed to help you think about big elements of your business, from your overall brand positioning to what products and services you offer. By reviewing trends in relation to your business strategy overall, you can start to rethink the way that you approach your business and make the changes necessary to compete in the new world and ensure you are as unique as possible.

CASE STUDY: Imagine You Work
at a Dental Surgery Office...

Most of your patients come from referrals and you rely on dentists and family doctors to send their patients to you. Unfortunately, you also happen to be offering a type of service that 100% of your patients hope to *not* need.

Visiting your office is a sign that something went wrong, and there's usually going to be pain involved after they leave. How do you turn this short-term negativity in a long-term positive experience that they will recommend to others?

At least you have the benefit of necessity on your side. Chances are, everyone who comes to see you really *needs* to see you. Keeping this in mind, how could trends shape the strategy of your business when you offer such a straightforward service that is mainly promoted through the willingness of other doctors to refer their patients to you?

The first key is deciding which trends to start your workshop brainstorming with, and the second is to develop valuable ideas for using them. Here are a few examples of how to do it based on three trends from this year's report:

1. **How to Use *Microconsumption*** – The same principle of a comedy club charging per laugh, could apply to your services as well. For example, what if you offered a price and time guarantee that patients would be able to get back to work within four hours of seeing you or you would give them a discount? Or,

you could partner with a valet car service and charge customers a small premium for a VIP drop-off service. The main point of this trend is rather than paying in one lump sum, patients are becoming accustomed to different payment models that take money in bursts and provide better value in the process.

2. **How to Use *Selfie Confidence*** – The culture of instant sharing means that you will have some patients who want to share what they can about an experience as it happens. The problem is, getting dental surgery is rarely a high-confidence moment. So how could you change this? One way could be to let patients use an app like Facetune while in your waiting room to create an image of what their new smile will eventually look like. Another could be to use interesting displays and backdrops in your office to encourage sharing while allowing these selfies to feature more of the background and less of themselves.

3. **How to Use *Mood Matching*** – Using the well-documented impact of mood on how people perceive an experience is a powerful trend to consider in the context of a dental surgery office. For example, what shades do you paint the walls to put patients at ease? How can you get them into a good mood when they first see you so they will be more likely to remember the overall experience as being less unpleasant or painful than they expected? Answering these questions alone could have a big impact.

RESOURCES:Where Can I Learn More about Business Strategy?

To build or rethink your business strategy, here are a few of my favorite resources to use and recommend to others:

- ***Business Model Generation* by Alexander Osterwalder and Yves Pigneur** – This highly useful, illustrated book is a collection of insights co-created by 470 practitioners, and features lots of helpful charts, diagrams and methodologies. It is the ultimate reference book for business models—not to be read cover to cover, but rather more useful if you flip through and look for ideas to inspire you serendipitously.

- *Positioning* **by Al Ries and Jack Trout** – Though a modern business classic, this book remains one of the most powerful and actionable books that you will ever read about developing a brand positioning, go-to-market strategy and standing out in the marketplace. It needs to be on your bookshelf if it isn't already.

- *Different* **by Youngme Moon** – Few business books are simultaneously profound, useful and beautifully written—but this one qualifies. Built around a fundamentally simple idea that the key to success is being different, popular Harvard professor Youngme Moon shares a surprisingly unique point of view on one of the most commonly discussed ideas in business.

For an online list featuring these resources and many more, please visit the link below:

WWW.ROHITBHARGAVA.COM/NONOBVIOUS/RESOURCES

HOW TO USE A CORPORATE CULTURE TREND WORKSHOP

.———.

> "IF YOU GET THE CULTURE RIGHT,
> EVERYTHING ELSE WILL FLOW NATURALLY."
> —TONY HSEIH, CEO of Zappos

It's never been a better time to be an employee.

Every week there are new stories of companies outdoing one another with new benefits designed to make them a friendly and more generous place for people to work.

Starbucks recently announced a new program to pay a portion of college expenses for baristas. Nestle has built an ambitious eight-month training program in digital marketing to inspire high performers and potential leaders. Nearly every major Silicon Valley tech company offers everything from free food to in-house massages in a desperate attempt to hold onto their best people.

All of these may seem like only the trappings of a real company culture, but they are powerful symbols of a new reinvestment from business into employees and the internal culture of an organization. In this chapter, you will learn some techniques for assessing your current corporate culture and using trends to think differently about how to inspire your workforce, or be inspired if you happen to *be* part of that workforce.

What Is Corporate Culture?

For all the talk about corporate culture, it can be widely misunderstood as simply the policies and guidelines that are in place for employees. Culture is more than a list of dos and don'ts.

There is a reason Zappos has become the *de facto* standard of an amazing corporate culture. Not only do employees of the brand contribute to a *Culture Book* hundreds of pages long, but they are widely known to be so fanatical about getting the culture fit right that they offer a cash incentive for newly hired employees to leave if the fit *isn't* right.

Does your business invest that type of time and attention toward getting the right people and creating a culture to keep them? It is a worthwhile question to ask, but very difficult to imagine how to affect in ways that are not too complex or costly to implement.

The workshop models shared in this chapter will tackle that issue from the angle of new trends shifting how employees connect (or don't) with the brands they work for. By understanding the trends, you can start to focus your thinking on how to improve very specific aspects of your culture—and realize the benefits in terms of being a more desirable place to work and retaining your best team members.

OBJECTIVE:
When Should You Use This Workshop?

There is no bad time to focus on corporate culture, however it may be more urgent for you if you are in a situation where you are about to hire a significant number of new employees or, perhaps, if you have a leadership change or several employees who have left within a short period of time.

Rethinking a corporate culture can also be a wonderful way of inspiring more productivity, getting the best out of the people you already have on a team, and just creating a more positive daily working experience for everyone involved.

PREPARATION:
What to Do Before the Workshop?

The best input before launching this workshop is always to start by collecting some feedback about your existing culture, both from employees and, perhaps, customers as well. You might choose to use a survey or questionnaire, or hold some sort of roundtable event to listen to suggestions or descriptions of your current culture.

Whichever method you choose, here are a few sample questions you might consider using to evaluate your current culture, and they are equally valuable if you can use and answer them honestly for yourself:

- Do you know what the company stands for and do you believe in that mission?
- Do you feel like you have the tools and skills required to do your job every day?
- Do you feel that you are trusted to do your job independently?
- Would you recommend our business as a place for your friends to work?
- Do you generally like your coworkers?

As you have no doubt noticed, most of these questions are designed to get an employee to evaluate a corporate culture based on empowerment, camaraderie and belief in the company's overall mission.

Aside from this informal approach, if you want to take a more detailed look at your corporate culture in preparation for a workshop, here are some of the best online tools and assessments you could use beyond the relatively simple method of a question-based survey:

- **Culture That Works (www.culturethatworks.net)** - A simple and easy-to-use downloadable individual assessment test from organizational culture consultants Jamie Notter and Maddie Grant.

- **The Oz Principle (www.ozprinciple.com)** – This companion website to a trio of best-selling books on corporate culture features a vast array of free online resources, webinars, software and extended information on how to assess and improve your corporate culture.

- **Zappos Insights (www.zapposinsights.com)** – This site has plenty of resources from Zappos, including the *Culture Book*, webinars and other free advice on how to assess your culture.

PARTICIPANTS:
Who Should Be Involved?

This workshop focuses on methods to use trends as a framework for creating a stronger employee corporate culture. As a result, it is usually valuable to have the right combination of influencers and implementers, as they will have ideas for how to change the culture, and also be in a position to help evangelize any changes or ideas that come out of the workshop as well.

Using this method, here is a suggested list of participants:

1. **Facilitator (1)** – The facilitator is the leader of the conversation and is responsible primarily for keeping the session on track, posing big questions, probing further when needed, ensuring no single participant dominates and summarizing the session and some of the discussion's big takeaways.

2. **Scribe (1)** – The point of having the task of recording notes separated from the facilitator is so the facilitator is free to focus on the conversation. The scribe, however, must do more than simply record what is said. He or she needs to be able to apply enough insight to capture the essence of ideas and connect them in real time.

3. **Corporate Culture Head (1)** – For any corporate culture to be evangelized and focused on, someone needs to take the responsibility to own it. For some organizations, this may be the leader of the entire company, and for others there may be a formal or informal role for someone to take on the

challenge of being a chief culture officer. It is vital to nominate this person before the workshop and ensure he or she is participating in it.

4. **Employees (2–4)** – In order to maintain a realistic point of view and evaluate ideas against the real life situation of your business, it is important to have some unbiased employee participants in this workshop. The ideal employees are confident enough to voice their opinions directly, and also influential enough that they will be able to command their co-workers' respect as they share the ideas from the workshop.

FORMAT: How Should the Workshop Be Structured?

If focusing on corporate culture is a relatively new topic for you or your colleagues, this may seem like a tough topic to get people to take seriously. With all the other important things that everyone has to worry about, the first challenge with setting up a workshop about corporate culture is to make sure that all the participants see and understand the importance of holding it.

Aside from this initial hurdle, the effectiveness of the workshop will be greatly improved if there is a strong structure in place to run it. To that end, here are two models that I have used in the past that may be worth considering:

1. **"Rethinking Hiring" Corporate Culture Trend Workshop** – Great cultures start (or continue) by hiring great people, so clearly the first place to start this type of workshop is with the process for how you recruit, interview and hire new team members. Is this process scripted? Does it vary by position type? Do you use external help? These sorts of questions can help you build a process flow for how you typically hire. Then, you can start to think about the trends that may impact each step of your recruiting and hiring process and how to use them.

2. **"Living The Mission" Corporate Culture Trend Workshop** – No matter the vision and mission behind your company, the obvious first step is to have a great articulation of it that everyone understands. Trends, however, can have an impact on how likely employees are to believe it, or how you might go about evangelizing it. Therefore, in this workshop, the focus is on taking the mission and using trends to make it more powerful, urgent, necessary and desirable, giving everyone more compelling reasons to believe in it.

RESULTS:
What Is the Benefit of the Workshop?

So many organizations have never really focused on building a powerful corporate culture, and this offers the chance to finally correct that oversight while still using the trends as a backdrop for what to shift and why. More importantly, if you can come out of a workshop about corporate culture with a new way to share that mission with your employees by leveraging the latest trends, you will be poised to help your business be even more effective and bring on stronger talent in the coming year.

CASE STUDY: Imagine You Work at
a Software Services Company

Standing out in a crowded market where there are several other companies offering similar services is your biggest challenge. You have plenty of technical experts at your company, but you're in an industry that faces rapid turnover and your competitors are ready to poach your best people at any moment.

Adding to the complexity is the fact that you have multiple locations and more than half of your employees have been with the company for less than two years. The good news is you have a founder who is still engaged with the company, and people are generally happy with the work that they do.

How do you take a nascent corporate culture and apply some of the latest 2015 trends to rethink how to engage employees to build a stronger culture for your software services company? Here are some specific ideas to illustrate what you might do:

1. **How to Use *Experimedia*** – When media increasingly features real life situations and social experiments to illuminate our behavior and how things work – it presents an opportunity to do the same in your software business. Rather than technical manuals or boring PowerPoint webinars, why not record and share live video of willing customers learning your product and using it in real life? Not only do "day in the life of" videos engage people on a different level, they also help you stand out by humanizing your product through featuring the people behind it.

2. **How to Use *Engineered Addiction*** – Instead of trying to get customers addicted to your software, you could use some of the principles of addictive design to improve the user experience. Rethinking your onboarding process for new customers could also generate similar benefits by hooking users on the simplicity or functionality of your solution right from the first moment they use it.

RESOURCES: Where Can I Learn More about Corporate Culture?

In addition to the resources shared earlier in this chapter, here are a few more that I have found particularly valuable to understanding the importance of building a powerful corporate culture:

- *Let My People Go Surfing* by **Yvon Chouinard** – Far before corporate culture was even a topic people discussed, Patagonia founder Yvon Chouinard was building a mission-driven organization with passionate employees. Today, his lessons and insights are even more valuable.

- *The Carrot Principle* **by Adrian Gostick and Chester Elton** – There is a reason this book is a classic in the world of leadership and corporate culture. The number-one reason people leave a job is because they don't feel appreciated. This book is filled with valuable reminders and ideas for how to create an empowered and supported workforce that always feels valued.

- *Taking People with You* **by David Novak** – This book crosses between leadership and corporate culture, but when you consider that the author runs a company that employs more than 1.4 million people globally (Yum! Brands), his insights are worth considering. This book is a surprisingly useful collection of tips and tricks from a field CEO who has spent his career leading in person rather than from the boardroom. That alone makes this book worth reading.

For an online list featuring these resources and many more, please visit the link below:

WWW.ROHITBHARGAVA.COM/NONOBVIOUS/RESOURCES

THE 7 BEST TREND RESOURCES
YOU NEED TO BOOKMARK

Despite the skepticism with which I often approach trend reports from so-called gurus, there are actually quite a few amazingly valuable sources for trend forecasting and techniques that I have drawn upon heavily over the years. Some have already been cited elsewhere in this book, however in the interests of simplicity, I am including a full list of some of my favorite resources below. (*Note:* Several top sources such as Iconoculture have been omitted from this list because most of their research is accessible only to subscribers and not the general public.)

These organizations and individuals publish consistently insightful ideas and forecasts worth paying attention to. Each is on my must-read list every year and never fails to offer several ideas that inform my thinking annually as I prepare the *Non-Obvious Trend Report.*

1. **Trendwatching.com (trendwatching.com)**
This is hands-down the most useful trend and forecasting resource in existence. Through a network of thousands of spotters all over the world, this is the one resource that I consistently find insightful, valuable and extremely well researched. There are several times, in fact, when seeking sources for a potential trend on my list turns up a very similar idea from Trendwatching.com. Visit their site and subscribe to receive their excellent free monthly reports. If you work for an organization that can

afford it, pay to access their premium service (currently $199 per month) and use it.

2. PSFK (www.psfk.com)

Ever since I first met founder Piers Fawkes at an event more than five years ago, I am consistently impressed with the thinking that he and his team compile on big topics like the future of retail and the future of work. Several of their reports are published in partnership with sponsors, which means they are freely available, but even just browsing their consistently excellent blog will inspire you with new ideas, curated observations and plenty of stories worth saving for later aggregation.

3. *Megatrends* by John Naisbitt

There is a reason why this is the book about trends and the future has been a bestseller for the past three decades. In the book, Naisbitt not only paints a fascinating future portrait of the world as he saw it back in the early '80s, but he also captures his own time in the mirror from the viewpoint he writes from. Despite the many years that have passed since the book was first published, it remains a valuable read both for the prescience of his ideas and the how he manages to capture the spirit of his time while comparing it to a surprisingly accurate vision of the future.

4. *The Trend Forecaster's Handbook* by Martin Raymond

There isn't really a textbook for trend forecasting, but if there were, this full-color large-format volume from Martin Raymond would come pretty close. It has a hefty price tag (like most textbooks), but the content is beautifully organized and it comes closest to presenting a dictionary-style compilation of everything you can imagine needing to know about trend forecasting. From interviews with top futurists to highly useful sidebars (like how to select and interview an expert panel), this book compiles so much insight that it's worth buying because you'll probably refer to it again and again.

5. Cool Hunting (www.coolhunting.com)

If you have ever been to one of those beautifully authentic farmer's markets where the produce is amazingly fresh, but the organization is a big haphazard and confusing – then you'll appreciate the value of Cool Hunting. The site has amazing content and is guaranteed to spark new ideas for you anytime you visit, but you'll have to navigate the busy design and minimal organization alongside those sparks of brilliance. If you can find the patience to browse the site instead of searching, though, you will find the content to be completely inspirational.

6. The Cool Hunter (www.thecoolhunter.co.uk)

Despite its name, this site has no affiliation with Cool Hunting. Aside from sharing a compendium of ideas, the structure of the sites couldn't be more different. On The Cool Hunter, all the blog posts are cleanly presented in very specific categories from "Exotic Places" to "Architecture." Each post is highly visual and it is easy to browse from story to story. As a result, the experience of navigating the site is a bit like going to a perfectly organized library and pulling random ideas off the shelf.

7. SlideShare (www.slideshare.com)

Almost every flawed, lazy or overly ambitious trend report I have ever read was one I found on Slideshare.com, so it probably seems like an odd choice to add to my list of must-read resources, but the fact is you can get a lot of great insights on SlideShare. Some of them relate to trend predictions that are of little value, but learning to *see through* them is a valuable skill in itself. Outside of that, there are plenty of deep, insightful presentations that can offer ideas about new industries and markets, or take you inside an unfamiliar subject in a visual and easy-to-read way.

For an online list of all the sources included here, please visit the link below:

WWW.ROHITBHARGAVA.COM/NONOBVIOUS/RESOURCES

ANTI-TRENDS:
The Flip Side Of Trends

"THERE ARE TRIVIAL TRUTHS AND THERE ARE GREAT TRUTHS.
THE OPPOSITE OF A TRIVIAL TRUTH IS PLAINLY FALSE. THE
OPPOSITE OF A GREAT TRUTH IS ALSO TRUE."

—NEILS BOHR, Nobel Prize-winning physicist

From the end of September until the beginning of November, the Piedmont region of Italy is one of the most popular destinations in the world for serious foodies. While the famous Barolo wines produced from the native Nebbiolo grape are an ongoing attraction, the main draw comes during the first week of October, when the town of Alba hosts its annual White Truffle Fair.

Truffles have become the ultimate decadent ingredient at fine restaurants around the world, and white truffles are the rarest—sometimes costing as much as $2000 per pound. Truffles from Alba are alternately described by chefs as "sublime" and "unlike anything else in the world." The Barolo wines for years have been considered Italy's best, called the "king of wines" for centuries.

As amazing a destination Piedmont seems, there is one interesting problem the region can't control: the weather.

Truffles are best after a wet summer, while wine is best after a dry and hot summer. As a result, any summer cannot be equally good for both wine *and* truffles.

Flip Thinking and Anti-Trends

In this book, I have shared a process for uncovering trends that affect the world around us, and advice on how to use them to power your business and career. Perhaps while reading one of these trends, you thought of an example that seemed to do the exact opposite of what the trend was describing.

These cases are always present. Like when reading about *Selfie Confidence*, you might also come across articles about how youth and others are using selfies to engage in another form of narcissistic behavior that helps no one. When considering the trend of *Glanceable Content*, you might be reminded of online destinations like Medium.com and Longform.org, which celebrate engaging longer articles.

Just like Piedmont's truffles and wine, there is an opposing force that balances out most trends in time, and it comes from people and companies that see what everyone else is doing and choose to do the opposite. Sometimes we hear it called "flip thinking," a term used most popularly by author Dan Pink. In one instance, he used it to describe a teacher who flipped the classroom by assigning math lectures via YouTube video as homework and actually doing the problems together in class.

Flip thinking will always be present, and for every trend the truth is someone will usually be able to find an example of the exact opposite. If we have invested all this work into curating and describing trends, how can we be sure they are actually valuable when it seems so easy to disprove them?

Breaking Trends

Trends are not like mathematical theories. They are describing something that is accelerating and will matter more and more, but they are not hard and fast rules of culture or behavior. There will always be outliers.

The point of curating trends is to see what others don't to predict a future that still has value even if it can never describe 100% of every situation. There is an interesting opportunity, though, that arises from being able to use this principle of flip thinking for yourself.

Understanding trends not only empowers you to use them positively, but also to intentionally break them and do the opposite when it's an appropriate way to stand out.

Pablo Picasso famously advised that each of us should aim to "learn the rules like a pro so you can break them like an artist."

The clown in an ice-skating show often needs to be the most talented in order to execute fake jumps and falls while still remaining under control, just like your ability to know the trends may give you the insight you need to bend or break them strategically.

This is, after all, a book about thinking in new and different ways. Taking a trend and aiming to embrace its opposite certainly qualifies.

AFTERWORD

"THERE'S NO SUCH THING AS WEIRD FOOD. ONLY WEIRD PEOPLE."

—FERRAN ADRIÀ, chef and molecular gastronomist

Apparently, the world will end on March 16, 2880.

While putting the final touches on this book, I came across a news article about a team of scientists who discovered a 0.3% chance the world will end on that day due to a cosmic collision course between the Earth and celestial body known only as Asteroid 1950 DA.

The story immediately struck me as the perfect metaphor for the types of predictions we commonly encounter … overblown proclamations with dire consequences and relatively little certainty.

One of my aims throughout this book was to challenge the lazy or obvious trend predictions that are published each year. They are sadly similar to this exaggerated astronomical example in terms of how much value they offer us in the present.

A trend is a unique curated observation of the accelerating present.

So this book very specifically *doesn't* offer geopolitical arguments for why Denmark is going to become the world's next superpower by 2050 thanks to wind energy production, or optimistic technology predictions about how self-driving cars will enable virtual-reality tourism during daily commutes.

I know those kinds of predictions are sexy, and some might even come true thanks to pure chance. Unfortunately, they also include a lot of uncertainty. Getting better at observing reality means preparing for the future should involve far less guesswork.

Curating trends is certainly about seeing the things other don't. Yet it is also more broadly about a mindset that encourages you to be curious and thoughtful. It is about techniques that help you move from trying to be a speed reader to being a speed *understander*, as Isaac Asimov would say.

I believe the future belongs to those who can learn to use their powers of observation to see the connections between industries, ideas and behaviors and curate them into a deeper understanding of the world around us.

I'm not saying that type of thinking can save us from the asteroid 867 years from now – but it can definitely change the way we approach our lives and our businesses in the present.

Preparing for the future starts with understanding *today*, as it always has.

ACKNOWLEDGEMENTS

Every author says that writing a book is rarely a solitary act. I have to disagree.

Along the past five years of journeying through the publishing industry—I have written books for large publishers as an author under contract, and I have self published short ebooks written alone in a couple of weeks.

Some come faster than others—and require a different team to put them together. Of them all, this book was the most complex, requiring more than a year's worth of research, writing and curation. The concept for the book was five years in the making, and the inspiration to write it came directly from the many people who have read one of my Non-Obvious Trend Reports and decided to get in touch and interact with me directly.

As much as anyone, this book is for them—and if you happen to be one of them I want to thank you first.

Beyond this broad group, there are also some individuals who helped with various stages of getting this book ready for publication and deserve my specific thanks:

First of all, to Matthew for being a sounding board on the editorial process and choosing to take on the editing of a project like this even though you've clearly moved on to bigger and better things.

To Herb for helping me navigate the ins and outs of the publishing industry and making exactly the kinds of connections that help a small independent publishing house with just a few authors grow to become something even bigger.

To Christina for her careful reading of an initial manuscript and fast work to make the words and ideas better without needing much space or time within which to do it.

Jeff, Kelly, Torrey and the entire design team at Faceout for understanding the concept of the book, working to translate that into a beautiful cover design, and being overall pleasant people to work with.

Rich for being a great partner, always working under a crazy timeline and still getting things done like a pro.

To my wife Chhavi, who continually manages to share interesting ideas, challenge me to reinvent my thinking, and cheerfully deal with a writing process that requires me to sometimes disappear to finish off chapters and "visualize" ideas by spreading my notes across entire rooms of the house. It is easy to write books and share ideas when you are married to someone who inspires you.

And finally, to my boys Rohan and Jaiden for remaining curious enough about the world to motivate me to observe more, judge less and always listen with both ears.

From time to time, we all need a reminder like that.

NOTES, REFERENCES, & CREDITS

‗—‗

The following is a comprehensive list of sources that were used in the preparation of this book, including all the articles, books and research that were consulted or cited. Where personal interviews were conducted, those have been individually cited within the relevant chapters and are not included separately in this final reference section.

For an online list of all the articles included here as well as live links to the original sources, please visit the link below:

WWW.ROHITBHARGAVA.COM/NONOBVIOUS/RESOURCES

INTRODUCTION
- http://www.nytimes.com/books/97/03/23/lifetimes/asi-v-obit.html

CHAPTER 1
- http://www.leadersmag.com/issues/2014.2_Apr/Norway/LEAD-ERS-Christian-Ringnes-Eiendomsspar-Victoria-Eiendom.html
- http://www.gonorway.no/norway/articles/4569
- https://storify.com/BeckiePort/overlyhonestmethods
- http://brandedcontent.adage.com/pdf/PR_Factor_online.pdf
- www.medium.com

CHAPTER 2
- http://www.powerhousemuseum.com/insidethecollection /2012/05/what-does-a-curator-really-do-in-a-day/
- *Curationism: How Curating Took Over the Art World and Everything Else* by David Balzer
- *The Greatest Stories Never Told: 100 Tales from History to Astonish, Bewilder, and Stupefy* by Rick Beyer
- http://en.wikipedia.org/wiki/Leif_Erikson
- http://mentalfloss.com/article/33584/ he-could-have-discovered-america-he-wanted-see-his-parents
- http://www.ptonline.com/articles/all-plastic-paint-cans-challenge-steel

- http://www.bloomberg.com/news/2014-12-22/coca-cola-disconnects
  -voice-mail-at-headquarters.html
- http://www.virgin.com/richard-branson/
  why-were-letting-virgin-staff-take-as-much-holiday-as-they-want
- http://www.copyblogger.com/removing-blog-comments/
- http://www.bbc.com/news/science-environment-29885832#story
  _continues_3
- http://www.karplab.net/news

CHAPTER 3

- http://www.rohitbhargava.com/2006/08/5_rules_of_soci.html
- http://usatoday30.usatoday.com/money/books/2006-09-24-naisbitt
  -usat_x.htm

CHAPTER 4: *EVERYDAY STARDOM*

- http://www.polygon.com/2013/12/14/5208764/batman-eric-johnston
  -batkid-make-a-wish-san-francisco
- http://sf.wish.org/wishes/wish-stories/i-wish-to-be/wish-to-be-batkid
- http://www.usatoday.com/story/news/nation/2013/11/15/batkid
  -san-francisco/3588173/
- http://batkidbegins.com/
- http://www.ibtimes.com/bollywood-100-how-big-indias-mammoth
  -film-industry-1236299
- http://www.timescrest.com/society/the-matrimony-matinee-7053
- http://contentmarketinginstitute.com/2011/08/museum-of-me/
- http://www.nytimes.com/2013/08/06/science/seeing-narcissists
  -everywhere.html?pagewanted=all
- http://www.nytimes.com/2015/01/15/style/be-the-star-of-your-own
  -snapchat-story-.html?_r=0

CHAPTER 5: *SELFIE CONFIDENCE*

- http://www.salon.com/2013/10/02/my_embarrassing_picture_went_viral/
- http://www.bullyingstatistics.org/content/cyber-bullying-statistics.html
- http://www.danah.org/name.html
- http://www.today.com/health/selfie-esteem-teens-say-selfies-give
  -confidence-boost-2D12164198
- http://www.mommyish.com/2014/01/22/selfie-documentary-shows
  -moms-influence-self-image/
- http://www.slate.com/articles/double_x/doublex/2013/11/selfies_on
  _instagram_and_facebook_are_tiny_bursts_of_girl_pride.html
- http://www.aol.com/article/2014/02/24/loveyourselfie/20836450/
- *It's Complicated: The Social Lives of Networked Teens* by danah boyd

- http://www.theatlantic.com/technology/archive/2014/06/everything-we
-know-about-facebooks-secret-mood-manipulation-experiment/373648/Ds
- https://medium.com/message/what-does-the-facebook-experiment
-teach-us-c858c08e287f
- http://www.cnn.com/2013/01/13/opinion/hancock-technology-lying/
- http://online.liebertpub.com/doi/abs/10.1089/cyber.2011.0389
- http://sml.comm.cornell.edu/wordpress/
- http://www.theselflessselfieproject.com/
- http://www.psfk.com/2014/10/uniquo-3dselfie-holiday-campaign
-selflessness.html
- http://www.entrepreneur.com/slideshow/239015

CHAPTER 6: *MAINSTREAM MINDFULNESS*

- http://www.nytimes.com/2014/02/05/sports/football/title-for-the
-seahawks-is-a-triumph-for-the-profile-of-yoga.html
- http://www.wired.com/2013/06/meditation-mindfulness-silicon-valley/all/
- http://www.businessweek.com/printer/articles/230076-thync-lets-you
-give-your-mind-a-jolt
- http://techcrunch.com/2014/05/30/headspace-releases-new-version-of
-its-meditation-platform/
- http://www.theguardian.com/guardian-masterclasses/2014/dec/23/an
-introduction-to-mindfulness-for-professionals
- https://hbr.org/2014/12/mindfulness-mitigates-biases-you-may-not
-know-you-have
- http://www.theguardian.com/sustainable-business/google-meditation
-mindfulness-technology
- http://www.newrepublic.com/article/120669/2014-year-mindfulness
-religion-rich
- http://www.mindful.org/sites/default/files/Mindful_freemium.pdf
- http://espn.go.com/nfl/story/_/id/9581925/seattle-seahawks-use
-unusual-techniques-practice-espn-magazine
- http://siyli.org/programs/
- http://www.ibisworld.com/industry/pilates-yoga-studios.html
- http://www.npr.org/2012/01/03/144627631/facebooks-bejar-takes-on
-compassion-challenge
- http://www.nytimes.com/2014/10/23/fashion/Facebook-Arturo-Bejar
-Creating-Empathy-Among-Cyberbullying.html?_r=0
- https://www.headspace.com/how-it-works
- http://mariashriver.com/blog/2013/11/how-i-did-it-ingrid-sanders
-founder-ceo-popexpert-daniel-jenks/
- http://mindfulnessinschools.org/

CHAPTER 7: *BRANDED BENEVOLENCE*

- http://www.toms.com/corporate-responsibility
- http://www.conversantip.com/blog/is-tesla-giving-up-its-patents-nope-elon-musk-is-offering-a-cross-license/
- http://www.teslamotors.com/blog/all-our-patent-are-belong-you
- http://www.businessweek.com/articles/2014-06-12/why-elon-musk-just-opened-teslas-patents-to-his-biggest-rivals
- http://www.cnbc.com/id/101701887#.
- https://www.youtube.com/watch?v=ts_4vOUDImE
- http://www.businessweek.com/stories/2006-05-07/suns-big-open-source-bet
- http://www.nielsen.com/content/corporate/us/en/insights/news/2014/it-pays-to-be-green-corporate-social-responsibility-meets-the-bottom-line.html
- http://www.accenture.com/SiteCollectionDocuments/PDF/Accenture-Consumer-Study-Marketing-Mattering.pdf
- http://insights.fb.com/2014/11/18/a-favorite-place-to-hang-out/
- http://www.cvshealth.com/research-insights/health-topics/this-is-the-right-thing-to-do

CHAPTER 8: *REVERSE RETAIL*

- http://www.businessinsider.com/reverse-showrooming-bricks-and-mortar-retailers-fight-back-2-2014-2
- http://www.hemispheresmagazine.com/2014/03/01/red-carpet-retail/
- https://hbr.org/product/how-pinterest-puts-people-in-stores/an/F1307Z-PDF-ENG
- http://www.entrepreneur.com/article/239690
- http://www.wsj.com/articles/SB10001424052702304587704577334370670243032
- http://adage.com/article/digitalnext/retailers-showrooming-a-bad-thing/292167/
- http://bits.blogs.nytimes.com/2013/02/27/more-retailers-at-risk-of-amazon-showrooming/?_r=0
- http://www.huffingtonpost.com/jon-bird/embracing-showrooming_b_5999302.html
- http://www.geekwire.com/2014/walmart-com-chief-neil-ashe-says-showrooming-longer-dirty-word/
- http://www.crmbuyer.com/story/81323.html
- http://www.inc.com/rhett-power/drones-augmented-reality-no-lines-a-glimpse-into-the-future-of-retail.html
- http://www.emarketer.com/Article/Retailers-Look-Merge-Offline-Online-Shopping-Experiences-2014/1010812
- http://www.mechtron.com/blog/sell-the-retail-experience/

- http://www.fastcocreate.com/3037575/how-4-retailers-are-using-digital-and-mobile-to-create-a-more-seamless-shopping-experience
- https://hbr.org/2014/09/digital-physical-mashups/ar/1
- http://www.adweek.com/news/technology/meet-7-brands-are-building-future-digital-retail-through-innovation-labs-161470
- http://www-935.ibm.com/services/us/gbs/thoughtleadership/greaterexpectations/
- http://thisisstory.com/stories/styletech/
- http://www.wired.com/2014/11/ebays-plan-reinvent-retail-shopping-magic-mirrors/
- http://thecreatorsproject.vice.com/blog/tescos-using-virtual-reality-goggles-to-possibly-allow-people-to-buy-groceries-from-bed
- http://gajitz.com/worlds-first-virtual-grocery-store-now-open-in-south-korea/
- http://www.samsung.com/us/galaxy-experience/#Home
- http://www.psfk.com/2014/09/story-style-tech-pop-up-store.html
- http://www.customerexperiencereport.com/expert-edge/omnichannel-changing-retail-experience-forever/

CHAPTER 9: *THE RELUCTANT MARKETER*

- http://adage.com/article/cmo-strategy/end-marketing-procter-gamble/293918/
- http://adage.com/article/cmo-strategy/call-cmo-marketers-job-evolved-title/245189/
- http://blogs.wsj.com/accelerators/2014/06/03/jessica-livingston-why-startups-need-to-focus-on-sales-not-marketing/
- http://www.foundersspace.com/marketing-pr/how-to-not-waste-millions-on-your-startup%E2%80%99s-marketing/
- http://www.marketing-interactive.com/features/rethinking-the-cmo/
- http://digiday.com/brands/x1-shiv-singh-the-well-rounded-marketer/
- https://www.spencerstuart.com/research-and-insight/tomorrows-cmo-chief-magic-or-logic-officer-highlights
- http://www.economistgroup.com/leanback/the-next-big-thing/big-rethink-closing-david-rogers-columbia/
- http://www.russellreynolds.com/content/confronting-cmo-succession-gap-five-key-findings-improving-readiness-and-retention-future-ma
- http://www.thedrum.com/news/2012/04/25/marketing-dead-says-saatchi-saatchi-ceo
- http://www.strategy-business.com/article/07306?pg=all
- http://www.lego.com/en-us/aboutus/news-room/2011/september/lego-group-expands-top-management

- http://www.imaginepub.com/how-lego-capitalized-on-content-marketing

CHAPTER 10: *GLANCEABLE CONTENT*

- http://agelab.mit.edu/files/AgeLab_typeface_white_paper_2012.pdf
- http://www.monotype.com/blog/burlingame
- http://www.hollywoodreporter.com/news/steve-jobs-death-apple
  -calligraphy-248900
- http://www.thinkingwithtype.com/misc/type_lecture/Type_Lecture.pdf
- http://www.thinkingwithtype.com/misc/Beautiful_Books.pdf
- http://www.statisticbrain.com/attention-span-statistics/
- http://blog.mozilla.org/metrics/2010/04/05/firefox-page-load-speed
  -%E2%80%93-part-ii/
- http://www.theatlantic.com/technology/archive/2013/12/why-are
  -upworthy-headlines-suddenly-everywhere/282048/
- http://www.rohitbhargava.com/2014/10/oreo-social-media-strategy.html
- http://www.wired.com/2014/11/the-internet-of-me/
- http://www.demandmedia.com/content-solutions/
- http://www.wired.com/2009/10/ff_demandmedia/all/
- http://www.theguardian.com/media-network/media-network-blog/2012
  /mar/19/attention-span-internet-consumer
- http://www.theguardian.com/commentisfree/2013/nov/04/in-defence
  -of-clickbait
- http://contentsolutions.demandmedia.com/to-bait-or-not-to-bait-the
  -click-bait-debate/
- http://www.elle.com/life-love/society-career/the-skimm

CHAPTER 11: *MOOD MATCHING*

- http://freshome.com/2007/04/17/
  room-color-and-how-it-affects-your-mood/
- http://www.engadget.com/2015/01/04/zensorium-being/
- http://wallstcheatsheet.com/life/your-mood-is-contagious-how-sharing-on
  -social-media-influences-others.html/?a=viewall
- http://scopeblog.stanford.edu/2014/10/03/
  how-social-media-can-affect-your-mood/
- http://richardcoyne.com/2014/10/11/
  do-digital-media-influence-your-mood/
- http://www.businessinsider.com/
  apples-mood-based-ad-targeting-patent-2014-1
- http://www.huffingtonpost.com/good-news/
- http://blogs.adobe.com/digitalmarketing/personalization/marketers
  -mood-ring-mood-targeting-goes-mainstream/

- http://www.businessinsider.com/yahoo-acquired-aviate-search-2014-1
- http://adage.com/article/digital/microsoft-files-patent-ad-serving-tech-senses-mood/235336/
- http://psychcentral.com/news/2014/10/03/can-social-media-help-you-out-of-a-bad-mood/75680.html
- http://observer.com/2015/01/the-next-big-thing-what-you-need-to-know-about-in-2015/
- http://ei.yale.edu/ruler/
- http://ps4daily.com/2013/03/sony-dualshock-4-light-bar-can-add-emersion-to-gaming-in-the-dark/

CHAPTER 12: *EXPERIMEDIA*

- http://qz.com/74937/how-to-become-internet-famous-without-ever-existing/
- http://santiagoswallow.com/2013/04/15/self/
- http://www.estherhonig.com/#!before--after-/cvkn
- http://www.buzzfeed.com/ashleyperez/global-beauty-standards?bffb
- http://thecreatorsproject.vice.com/blog/we-talked-to-the-woman-who-asked-25-countries-to-photoshop-her-face
- http://www.mirror.co.uk/news/weird-news/pranksters-proposition-women-sex-1m-4458876
- http://youtu.be/n3M-ZlDdLzw
- http://www.today.com/health/paper-bag-speed-dating-event-tests-whether-love-blind-1D80307906
- http://news.prudential.com/article_display.cfm?article_id=6966

CHAPTER 13: *UNPERFECTION*

- http://www.businessweek.com/articles/2014-09-04/mining-okcupids-data-reveals-how-we-date-now
- http://blog.okcupid.com/index.php/race-attraction-2009-2014/
- http://abc13.com/society/ugly-christmas-sweaters-now-a-trend-/433411/
- http://newsfeed.time.com/2011/12/22/a-brief-history-of-the-ugly-christmas-sweater/
- http://www.nflshop.com/Ugly_Sweaters
- http://www.washingtonpost.com/blogs/style-blog/post/ugly-holiday-sweater-parties-the-origin-of-the-seasons-sarcastic-trend/2011/11/29/gIQAzl3g9N_blog.html
- http://www.uggaustralia.com/world-of-ugg-story.html
- http://www.economist.com/news/business/21592656-etsy-starting-show-how-maker-movement-can-make-money-art-and-craft-business
- http://www.businessweek.com/innovation/for-successful-innovation-sell-imperfect-products-01252012.html

CHAPTER 14: *PREDICTIVE PROTECTION*

- http://www.futurestructure.com/8-Mind-blowing-Uses-of-Wearable -Technology-Seriously.html
- http://www.ce.org/i3/Features/2014/January-February/Driverless-Cars-on -the-Rise.aspx
- http://thenextweb.com/google/2014/04/13/built-google-owned-wazes -biggest-asset-community/
- https://www.linkedin.com/pulse/20141021042240-8451-move-over -humans-the-robocars-are-coming
- http://www.slideshare.net/JavelinMktg/identity-fraud2014 -infographicjavelinstrategy
- https://www.javelinstrategy.com/brochure/314
- http://www.cbsnews.com/news/identity-theft-rises-consumers-rage/
- http://www.idtheftcenter.org/images/breach/ITRC_Breach_Report_2014.pdf
- https://www.etsy.com/shop/BohemianFindings
- http://www.craftcount.com/
- http://www.wired.com/2014/09/wrong-theory/
- http://www.npr.org/blogs/thesalt/2014/12/09/369613561/in-europe-ugly -sells-in-the-produce-aisle
- http://www.dailymail.co.uk/femail/food/article-2693000/Forget-ugli -fruit-meet-ugly-fruit-bowl-French-supermarket-introduces-lumpy -misshapen-fruit-vegetables-sold-30-discount-combat-food-waste.html
- http://www.washingtonpost.com/wp-srv/style/features/daily/rehm0823.htm
- http://grist.org/list/fast-food-giants-make-their-food-look-imperfect-so- youll-forget-its-hella-processed/

CHAPTER 15: *ENGINEERED ADDICTION*

- *Salt Sugar Fat* by Michael Moss
- *Hooked* by Nir Eyal
- *Addictive by Design* by Natasha Dow Schüll
- *Abundance* by Peter Diamandis and Steven Kotler
- http://pando.com/2013/09/02/curious-a-lesson-in-addictive-learning/
- http://thenextweb.com/dd/2014/10/28/10-ingredients-concoct -subconsciously-addictive-mobile-app/
- https://www.yahoo.com/tech/this-new-ios-app-could-cure-you-of-your -iphone-90357333444.html
- http://www.dailymail.co.uk/sciencetech/article-2814488/App-Offtime -people-addicted-smartphones.html
- http://www.wsj.com/articles/SB100014240527023038745045793763232711 10900

- http://www.usatoday.com/story/tech/gaming/2014/02/11/flappy-bird -creator/5388515/
- http://www.forbes.com/sites/stevenkotler/2012/08/27/want-to-make- millions-and-change-the-world-theres-a-huge-gap-in-the-education -market/
- http://marketing.wtwhmedia.com/new-harvard-study-shows-why-social -media-is-so-addictive-for-many/
- http://www.huffingtonpost.com/2014/12/13/social-media-addiction_n _6302814.html
- http://www.forbes.com/sites/rogerdooley/2014/02/26/hooked/
- http://www.nytimes.com/roomfordebate/2013/10/09/are-casinos-too -much-of-a-gamble/slot-machines-are-designed-to-addict
- http://www.themortonreport.com/entertainment/games/why-is-angry -birds-so-addictive-a-cognitive-teardown/
- http://www.vox.com/2014/8/7/5976927/slot-machines-casinos-addiction -by-design
- http://www.newrepublic.com/article/115838/gambling-addiction-why -are-slot-machines-so-addictive
- http://venturebeat.com/2013/07/08/behavior-enigineering/
- https://gigaom.com/2012/09/02/when-did-addiction-become-a-good-thing/
- http://www.polygon.com/2013/3/4/4051444/simcity-review
- http://www.nytimes.com/2013/02/24/magazine/the-extraordinary-science -of-junk-food.html?pagewanted=all&_r=0
- http://www.theatlantic.com/entertainment/archive/2014/08/swing -copters/379117/?single_page=true
- http://www.dailydot.com/gaming/psychology-flappy-bird-addiction/
- http://www.google.com/trends/2014/
- http://www.complex.com/pop-culture/2013/11/snacks-that-are-more -addictive-than-cocaine/starbursts
- https://www.khanacademy.org/badges
- http://www.fastcompany.com/3007951/tech-forecast/simple-khan -academy-interface-hack-improved-learning-5

CHAPTER 16: SMALL DATA

- http://www.zdnet.com/article/10-reasons-2014-will-be-the-year -of-small-data/
- http://www.theguardian.com/news/datablog/2013/apr/25/forget-big-data -small-data-revolution
- https://hbr.org/2013/12/you-may-not-need-big-data-after-all
- http://www.ibmbigdatahub.com/infographic/taming-big-data-small-data -vs-big-data

- http://www.huffingtonpost.com/brian-kibby/targeted-analytics_b_5534291.html
- http://www.wired.com/2013/03/the-importance-of-data-portability-and-data-apis/
- http://www.destinationcrm.com/Articles/Web-Exclusives/Viewpoints/5-Ways-Small-Data-Can-Be-More-Valuable-than-Big-Data-98927.aspx
- http://www.techopedia.com/definition/29539/small-data
- http://www.mediapost.com/publications/article/239102/whats-it-going-to-be-big-data-or-small-data.html
- http://www.cmswire.com/cms/big-data/big-data-is-getting-smaller-and-smarter-027280.php#null
- https://www.constellationr.com/content/internet-things-requires-big-data-be-turned-upside-down-become-smart-data
- http://www.informationweek.com/healthcare/analytics/personal-healthcare-big-data-great-small-data-better/a/d-id/1306954
- http://adage.com/article/digitalnext/small-big-data/296458/
- http://www.meetup.com/smalldata/
- http://www.knightfoundation.org/blogs/knightblog/2014/8/14/knight-mozilla-fellows-take-era-no-excuses-public-data-demands/
- http://www.theatlantic.com/technology/archive/2014/11/the-passages-that-readers-love/381373/
- http://www.vox.com/2014/6/8/5786196/7-things-the-most-highlighted-kindle-passages-tell-us-about-american
- http://blogs.dlapiper.com/privacymatters/global-internet-of-things-top-ten-data-protection-concerns/
- https://www.youtube.com/watch?v=d-4i2ZlqLsI
- http://www.huffingtonpost.com/2012/10/12/ian-mcleod-21-years_n_1961336.html

CHAPTER 17: *DISRUPTIVE DISTRIBUTION*

- http://www.core77.com/blog/case_study/csads_disruptive_distribution_model_lessons_from_the_inaugural_community-supported_art_design_initiative_call_for_proposals_extended_to_april_3rd_26537.asp
- http://www.wsj.com/articles/for-taylor-swift-the-future-of-music-is-a-love-story-1404763219
- http://www.smh.com.au/small-business/startup/which-industries-are-dying-20140623-3anyj.html
- http://www.businessweek.com/articles/2014-08-20/taylor-swifts-new-album-1989-breaks-no-rules-whatsoever
- http://bits.blogs.nytimes.com/2013/12/20/binging-on-beyonce-the-ripple-effect/?_r=0

- http://www.billboard.com/articles/news/6174827/weird-al-yankovic-reflects-on-his-weirdly-successful-week
- http://www.project-disco.org/competition/diy-with-vhx-like-ck-displacing-the-intermediaries/
- http://www.usatoday.com/story/money/business/2014/12/23/247-wall-st-dying-thriving-industries/20185247/
- http://www.washingtonpost.com/blogs/the-switch/wp/2014/10/22/why-tesla-keeps-fighting-for-direct-sales-when-it-could-just-work-with-dealers/
- https://us.drive-now.com/#!/howto
- http://www.businessweek.com/articles/2014-02-06/russian-web-retailer-lamoda-deploys-own-delivery-service
- http://www.ewdn.com/2014/09/05/lamoda-ru-merged-into-multibillion-dollar-global-fashion-e-commerce-group/
- http://rocketinternet.pr.co/69143-world-bank-group-s-ifc-invests-10-million-into-lamoda

CHAPTER 18: *MICROCONSUMPTION*

- http://www.businessweek.com/articles/2014-11-20/mobile-payment-startup-venmo-is-killing-cash
- http://www.thewire.com/culture/2014/04/why-the-venmo-newsfeed-is-the-best-social-network-nobodys-talking-about/361342/
- http://thefinancialbrand.com/43203/paypal-venmo-social-mobile-payments/
- http://www.washingtonpost.com/blogs/innovations/wp/2014/10/14/an-innovative-new-payment-model-thats-no-laughing-matter/
- http://metro.co.uk/2014/10/11/try-not-to-laugh-this-comedy-club-charges-you-by-how-much-you-enjoy-the-show-4901504/
- http://variety.com/2014/film/news/jeffrey-katzenberg-predicts-3-week-theatrical-window-in-future-1201166052/
- http://adage.com/article/media/digital-advertising-ready-ditch-click/295143/
- http://www.wired.com/2014/07/multi-screen-life/
- http://www.coindesk.com/tipping-point-bitcoin-micropayments/
- http://www.niemanlab.org/2014/09/netflix-joins-the-push-for-bite-sized-mobile-friendly-video/
- http://www.theguardian.com/media/2014/nov/06/economist-espresso-digital-briefing

CHAPTER 19

- http://rumchata.com/#/about/about-us
- http://issuu.com/barbusinessmagazine/docs/oct_2013_bar_business_magazine
- http://www.businessweek.com/articles/2014-10-09/rumchatas-success-is-game-changer-among-cream-liqueurs

- http://www.fastcompany.com/1739774/how-carrots-became-new-junk-food
- *The Click Moment* by Frans Johansson

CHAPTER 20 NOTES

- https://www.youtube.com/watch?v=mSxpVRo3BLg

CHAPTER 21 NOTES

- http://www.fastcompany.com/3002804/
  how-sell-1-snow-globe-59-real-roi-brand-storytelling
- http://significantobjects.com/

CHAPTER 25 NOTES

- http://content.time.com/time/magazine/article/0,9171,2029487,00.html
- http://ny.eater.com/2014/11/4/7151951/white-truffles-in-restaurants
- http://www.foodandwine.com/articles/is-barolo-still-italys-greatest-wine
- http://www.telegraph.co.uk/finance/businessclub/7996379/Daniel-Pinks
  -Think-Tank-Flip-thinking-the-new-buzz-word-sweeping-the-US.html

---

TREND ICON DESIGN CREDITS (From the Noun Project)

Chapter 4 "Everyday Stardom" - Icon Credit: "King" symbol by Luis Prado from the Noun Project

Chapter 5 "Selfie Confidence" - Icon Credit: "Selfie" symbol by Les viex garçons from the Noun Project

Chapter 6 "Mainstream Mindfulness" - Icon Credit: "Mental Health" symbol by Gemma Garner from the Noun Project

Chapter 7 "Branded Benevolence" - Icon Credit: "Charity" symbol by Ben Rizzo from the Noun Project

Chapter 8 "Reverse Retail" - Icon Credit: "In-Stock" symbol by Dmitry Orlov from the Noun Project

Chapter 9 "The Reluctant Marketer" - Icon Credit: "Help" symbol by Luis Prado from the Noun Project

Chapter 10 "Glanceable Content" - Icon Credit: "Eye-Device" symbol by David Carrero from the Noun Project

Chapter 11 "Mood Matching" - Icon Credit: "Customer-Satisfaction" symbol by Luis Prado from the Noun Project

Chapter 12 "Experimedia" - Icon Credit: "Museum Visit" symbol by Luis Prado from the Noun Project

Chapter 13 "Unperfection" - Icon Credit: "Leaning-Tower" symbol by iconsmind.com from the Noun Project

Chapter 14 "Predictive Protection" - Icon Credit: "Safety Goggles" symbol by Luis Prado from the Noun Project

Chapter 15 "Engineered Addiction" - Icon Credit: "Texting" symbol by Luis Prado from the Noun Project

Chapter 16 "Small Data" - Icon Credit: "Chart" symbol by Jonathan Higley from the Noun Project

Chapter 17 "Disruptive Distribution" - Icon Credit: "Collection" symbol by Kirill Ulitin from the Noun Project

Chapter 18 "MicroConsumption" - Icon Credit: "Windows" symbol by iconsmind.com from the Noun Project

APPENDICES

THE PAST YEARS' NON-OBVIOUS TREND REPORTS

(2011–2014)

OVERVIEW:
How to Read These Past
Trend Reports

———

"THE EVENTS OF THE PAST CAN BE MADE TO PROVE
ANYTHING IF THEY ARE ARRANGED IN A SUITABLE PATTERN."
—A. J. P. Taylor, historian and journalist

There was a moment several years ago when I was on stage after having just presented one of my trend reports and a gentleman stood up to ask me a question. "It must be easy," he started "to publish your trend report when you get to change them every year. How do you know whether any of them were actually right?"

His question was a fair one. After all, there is plenty of evidence to suggest experts routinely miss predictions and are often just plain wrong. What makes my method or the past trends any different? Of course, every author thinks his book is brilliant, just as all parents imagine their child to be a genius. What is the truth?

In this section, you'll see a candid, unedited review of every one of my previously predicted trends from the past four years of the *Non-Obvious Trend Report*. While some of the descriptions have been edited for space considerations, none of the intentions or meanings have been updated or revisited.

Instead, each trend is accompanied by my own Trend Longevity Rating, which aims to measure how much the trend, as originally described, still applies or has value today in 2015. Predictably, the 2014 trends fared better than the 2011 trends, but the process of going backward and taking an honest look at past research was illuminating for me, and I hope it will be for you as well.

In assessing these trends, my aim was to treat them in as unbiased a way as possible, and where something was wrong or not quite right, I tried to assess and grade it truthfully. For each trend report, there is also a link at the end of the corresponding appendix where you can go back and see that full trend report with no edits, as it was originally presented.

It may be a hard line, but I have done my best to draw it authentically and without embarrassment or defensiveness. If there is anything that has helped me get better at doing this year after year, it's the act of reviewing, grading and critiquing past trends—especially after some of them turn out to be not quite right. I hope you enjoy this journey back in time and the ideas it sparks for which trends stood the test of time and which didn't.

APPENDIX A: 2011 Trends

THE BACKSTORY

The first edition of the *Non-Obvious Trend Report* was inspired by five years of blogging. I released it exclusively in a visual presentation format and heavily featured marketing and social media trends that I had written about throughout 2010. The trends were far more limited in scope than later editions of the trend report and featured less description and less actionable advice. They were also not separated into subcategories, but instead presented as a full list of 15 marketing and social media trends that mattered. Each trend featured a short description, along with some quick tips for brands on how to use the lessons in the report to power their marketing strategy.

RETROSPECTIVE – HOW ACCURATE WAS THIS REPORT?

The report was one of the first to predict the rise in importance of content marketing through curation and also predicted the rapid growth of real-time customer service through social media. It analyzed the increasing number of marketing campaigns featuring employees as a sign of corporate humanity, and introduced the idea of how social media was making unreachable celebrities more connected and approachable. Overall, there were relatively few big misses or trends that completely imploded or reversed themselves. The biggest idea from the report was undoubtedly the first trend *Likeonomics*, which ultimately inspired me to write a book of the same name (released in 2012) to build the idea out further.

THE 2011 TRENDS:
RECAP AND ANALYSIS

1. **Likeonomics**

   Brands, products and services succeed by being more human, mission driven and personally likeable through their policies and people, gaining an advantage over less-human competitors.

   Examples Used: Ford Explorer Facebook launch and Innocent Drinks

   2015 Trend Longevity Rating: A

   The fundamental truth of human relationships underlying this trend continued to grow in business this past year as more brands focused on being more human, building personal connections with customers and trying to be more consistently likeable.

2. **Approachable Celebrity**

   As social media allows direct access to previously unreachable celebrities, politicians and professional athletes, we increasingly see their real personalities (for better or worse) and can engage with them as real people.

   Examples Used: Cisco's "Do You Flip?" campaign and tweeting celebrities

   2015 Trend Longevity Rating: A

   This direct connection to celebrities has continued to grow as YouTube creates more celebrities who have huge personal followings, and notable people from all industries continue to share their real personalities and opinions through social media without filters or PR spokespeople.

3. **Desperate Simplification**

   Information overload causes consumers to desperately seek simplicity, leading them to aim for more balance through reduction activities like de-friending and actively seeking out new products and sites to help them simplify everything.

Examples Used: iPod, Tumblr, Animoto, Amazon, and Path

2015 Trend Longevity Rating: B-

While "infobesity," as information overload is increasingly being called, continues, the desperate need for simplicity has given way somewhat to more tools that focus on optimizing or curating instead of just culling friendships or content. As a result, this trend continues to matter, but the level of desperation from consumers doesn't have the same intensity it once did in past years.

4. Essential Integration

Marketers' biggest problem continues to be integrating efforts, which can be highly difficult and lack good examples, yet the biggest successes of the past year, in terms of award-winning marketing programs, feature a new level of integration that is still rare in the marketing world.

Examples Used: Old Spice Guy and Best Buy's Twelpforce

2015 Trend Longevity Rating: B

Over the past four years, integration has become an even greater issue for marketers and one that most struggle with on a daily basis—yet there are also more tools and platforms enabling this to happen more easily. This makes it still a trend that matters, but one that is less urgent, problematic and lacking in solutions.

5. Rise of Curation

Brands increasingly use curation as a much-needed filter to help find and bring together useful or entertaining content in an effort to win more trust and attention from consumers.

Examples Used: Paper.li custom newspapers and the Pharma and Healthcare Social Media Wiki

2015 Trend Longevity Rating: A

The past four years have delivered an even bigger explosion in content. The algorithms are getting smarter but are not yet smart enough to collect content into truly meaningful arrangements. As a result, curation has become an even bigger part of the content marketing strategy for brands, as well as a method for individuals to share their expertise or passion about any topic online.

6. Visualized Data

To make sense of a real-time stream of information on any topic, more and more event managers, news organizations and brands are turning to visualization as a way to leverage their data, better understand it and tell a clearer story.

Examples Used: The 52nd Annual Grammy Awards and CNN's Magic Election Wall

2015 Trend Longevity Rating: B

While data visualization is still frequently used, the widespread overuse of infographics over the past several years has weakened the focus on visuals as a way of using data to tell stories. Instead, more companies are combining the idea of visualization with better user interfaces, gamified design and narrative data storytelling to broaden their methods for getting value out of analyzing data and making it more shareable.

7. Crowdsourced Innovation

Brands turn to crowdsourced platforms to collect ideas from consumers in exchange for the reward of recognition, financial earning and simply being heard by the brands they purchase from every day.

Examples Used: My Starbucks Idea and Kickstarter

2015 Trend Longevity Rating: B

With the growth of Quirky, Kaggle and other platforms for everything from idea generation to problem solving, this trend has certainly continued to grow. My original definition was narrow and focused on brands and consumers, but this has given way to larger ecosystems and marketplaces that exist today with only limited brand support or sponsorship.

8. Instant PR & Customer Service

Real-time contact becomes essential as communications teams focus on instant PR to manage social crises and augment customer service with methods for dealing with problems in the here and now.

Examples Used: JetBlue's big media hit and Zappos' Golden Philosophy

2015 Trend Longevity Rating: A

When I first wrote this trend, the idea of customer service through social channels was mostly driven by negative situations and the need for

instant PR. Over the past several years, this has exploded into social customer care, a field that almost every large business is investing dollars and time in to figuring out how to do right.

9. App-fication of the Web

As more innovative apps let consumers bypass the web for transactions and leisure, a large number of activities from online banking to online shopping will shift to apps instead of the web.

Examples Used: Flipboard "The Web Is Dead. Long Live the Internet" from *Wired* magazine.

2015 Trend Longevity Rating: C+

There is no denying that the prevalence of apps has grown dramatically over the past several years, but idea of "app-fication," where everything is done through apps, has not quite come to pass. Instead, responsive design and the focus on making everything work for multiple screens has made apps just one part of the overall multiscreen experience most consumers have.

10. Re-Imagining Charity

Brands and entrepreneurs create innovative new models for social good, reinventing how people can do everything from donating money to sharing time and specific skills.

Examples Used: Jumo and Yoxi.tv

2015 Trend Longevity Rating: B-

The year when I first spotlighted this trend was one where the pace of growth in how nonprofits and charities were using digital tools was explosive. This speed has slowed somewhat as many of these same organizations shifted from doing something completely new online to focusing on how to optimize their efforts and gain better results in more recent years.

11. Employees As Heroes

Brands of all sizes aim to demonstrate their humanity by putting a spotlight on employees as the solvers of problems and creators of innovation. Organizations feature employee stories as anchor points to describe what the company does in the world.

Examples Used: Intel's "Sponsors of Tomorrow" campaign and IBM's Smarter Planet initiative

2015 Trend Longevity Rating: B

The past few years have added several large brands to this trend beyond the (mostly) tech companies like Intel and IBM that I initially featured. Yet the hero aspect of it has dissipated somewhat as brands start to take a softer and more consumer-centric approach to spotlighting employees. Those same employees are still an important and human part of the brand story, but they are presented more often now in terms of how hard they work, what value they bring to customers and why they are passionate about what they do.

12. Locationcasting

More consumers choose to broadcast their locations, enabling brands to tailor messages to a specific location and create more opportunities to engage their customers in real life.

Examples Used: Foursquare, Gowalla and Scvnger.com

2015 Trend Longevity Rating: B-

Mobile marketing is growing rapidly, as are methods for geotargeting offers for customers. This still has not become a commonplace activity, though, and it will take time for consumers to get over their privacy concerns or fears of being geospammed as they walk down the street.

13. Brutal Transparency

Aggressive honesty will lead to edgier (and more effective) marketing as brands reveal an unexpected aggressive honesty that consumers welcome.

Examples Used: Domino's Pizza's "Oh Yes We Did" campaign and Southwest Airlines' policy to eliminate baggage fees

2015 Trend Longevity Rating: A-

The growth of social platforms and increase in content marketing is allowing brands to share more honest truths about every aspect of their business than ever before. Combined with that, customer expectations are growing around the basic level of transparency they expect and brands need to meet the demand—even if the truths shared don't seem quite as brutal as they may once have.

14. Addictive Randomness

Brands will increasingly use the addictive power of random content to engage consumers and this will lead to more consumer-generated campaigns where people can add content to a central archive that anyone can browse.

Examples Used: Red Cross' "Why the Heck Should I Give?" campaign and PostSecret.com

2015 Trend Longevity Rating: C

This principle still applies in a limited scope to campaigns featuring a random sort of interface or user experience, however it never quite became large enough to be truly considered a trend lasting far beyond 2011.

15. Culting of Retail

The best retailers create a passionate following of users who not only buy products they like, but also rave about their experiences so completely that they will inspire a significant portion of their social networks to try the experience for themselves.

Examples Used: Groupon and Gilt

2015 Trend Longevity Rating: A-

If anything, the rise of social media has enabled this culting of retail to happen even more frequently. New boutique services and websites pop up nearly every day, and the ones that survive rely on their most enthusiastic customers, whose willingness share their brand passion online influences others to become customers as well.

Want to Read the Full Report for Free?

Visit www.15trends.com to read and download the full report.

APPENDIX B: 2012 Trends

THE BACKSTORY

This second year of the trend report featured a broader look at business beyond marketing and brought together the worlds of corporate marketing, charitable causes, the marketing of death and more. Like the first report, it was only released exclusively in visual presentation format online. This report tackled the sensitive yet emerging field of the digital afterlife of loved ones who have passed on, as well as the rising sense of social loneliness that people felt. In contrast to my 2011 report, the theme of this one moved a little further away from marketing campaigns and took a more human tone as many of the trends featured cultural or consumer-based trends instead of those inspired by what brand marketers were already doing.

RETROSPECTIVE – HOW ACCURATE WAS THIS REPORT?

More than any other year, the 2012 report had a few big hits and several big misses. The overall trends that centered on the growth of humanity in companies and consumers worked out well. This report was one of the first to explore the potential of big data to impact everything from optimizing supply chain logistics to measuring and quantifying every aspect of our lives. On the flip side, the trends that made bigger bets on niche concepts like *Pointillist Filmmaking* or *Social Artivism* did not quantifiably catch fire, either in adoption or in the behaviors they described.

THE 2012 TRENDS: RECAP & ANALYSIS

1. Corporate Humanism

Companies find their humanity as they create more consumer-friendly policies and practices, spending more time listening to customers and encouraging employees to more publicly represent their companies.

Examples Used: Aviva, Ally Bank, Domino's Pizza and Best Buy

2015 Trend Longevity Rating: A

If there is one trend that perhaps describes the past decade of corporate evolution, it is this one. Every year there are new signs of how companies are finding their humanity and avoiding the facelessness that once used to be a hallmark of business.

2. Ethnomimicry

Ethnographic analysis of how people interact in the real world inspires new social tools or products that mimic human behavior and social interaction, and fit our lives.

Examples Used: Google+, Emotion Lighting and Microsoft Kinetic

2015 Trend Longevity Rating: B

I am keenly aware that any trend which used Google+ as an example can't be scored particularly high as a matter of principle, however this idea of companies watching human interaction in the real world and tailoring products and services to mimic those behaviors is still a common design principle and frequently results in valuable and useful products or services.

3. Social Loneliness

Despite online social connections, people feel a real-world sense of loneliness, causing them to seek deeper friendships instead of many superficial ones. As a result, people seek new ways of knowing friends beyond their latest tweet.

Examples Used: Toyota Venza's "This Is Living" campaign and Couchsurfing.com

2015 Trend Longevity Rating: B

This sense of social loneliness is still present with interactions online, and it is a concern particularly for teens and adolescents, but there is far greater awareness of the issue along with more innovation from startup products and services that connect the digital world more deeply with the real world.

4. Pointillist Filmmaking

Named after the painting form using millions of dots to create larger images, this trend describes a form of collaborative filmmaking where are large number of short clips are merged together in order to tell a broader story through video.

Examples Used: Mont Blanc's Beauty of a Second Challenge and One Day on Earth

2015 Trend Longevity Rating: C

This trend was an example of an overly fancy concept that ended up being too limited in scope to really become an impactful trend over the long term. The experience of writing this and reviewing it years later, though, was a perfect lesson in the importance of making sure that an idea is big enough to truly accelerate in subsequent years. This one was not.

5. Measuring Life

A growing range of tracking tools offer individualized data to monitor and measure all areas of your life to allow you to track your own health, measure your social influence and set goals.

Examples Used: Jawbone Up and Klout

2015 Trend Longevity Rating: A

What was a big idea back in 2012 is now mainstream as new wearable devices are seemingly launched every week and the Internet of Things dominates headlines among the many technology trends that matter for the future. While much of that growth to date has been in the areas of health and fitness, other industries are becoming more active and will be launching their own measurement and tracking devices the coming year.

6. Co-Curation

Curation gets more collaborative as amateurs and experts combine forces online to add their unique points of view and bring together multiple angles of every issue.

Examples Used: Storyful & Futurity

2015 Trend Longevity Rating: B+

Curation continued to be one of the biggest trends in online content over the past few years, however this idea of co-curation and the central role of collaboration as a part of curation activities online never quite dominated in the way that this trend predicted. Instead, tools make it easier for anyone to curate information more simply and individually without taking the extra time that collaboration sometimes requires.

7. Charitable Engagement

More charities rethink their focus on quick donations and instead actively promote participation through gaming and other methods of behavioral engagement.

Examples Used: WaterForward.org and Jamie Oliver's Food Revolution

2015 Trend Longevity Rating: B

While charities and nonprofits continue to find more ways to engage donors proactively in their efforts, this trend predicted a dramatic shift in the industry that didn't quite come to pass over the past several years. More platforms to allow for convenient donation collection and the ease of online publishing actually led more smaller nonprofits to focus on the fundraising side of the equation for the short term, and on engagement only in the longer term.

8. Medici Marketing

Inspired by the book *The Medici Effect*, this trend describes how thinking from multiple disciplines is combined to make marketing more engaging, creative or useful.

Examples Used: The Creators Project and Albam's *Factories* book

2015 Trend Longevity Rating: B+

The name was a bit limiting to describe the scope of this trend, however the idea that marketing was becoming more of a melting pot for

people from nontraditional backgrounds including journalism and art certainly has continued throughout the last several years and for the foreseeable future.

9. Digital Afterlife

Over the past year, more companies have started to focus on the digital afterlife, creating tools, education and services to help manage all the data that loved ones leave behind after they die.

Examples Used: 1000memories.com (since acquired by Ancestry. com) and Aftersteps.com

2015 Trend Longevity Rating: B

This is the perfect type of frustrating trend prediction, that always seems to be on the cusp of emerging as a mainstream idea but never quite makes it. Over the past several years, there is always a steady drumbeat of stories and attention on this idea of the digital afterlife, but it rarely translates into something bigger.

10. Real-Time Logistics

Tech-savvy businesses use real-time conversation in social media to generate insights that help with supply chain and logistical planning to eliminate wastage and maximize profits.

Examples Used: Walmart Labs and SAP's social supply chain

2015 Trend Longevity Rating: A

Supply chain software continues to get more and more sophisticated as large retailers and other distributors continue to implement new tools to get better forecasts and leverage social conversation data to run their businesses better.

11. Social Artivism

The intersection between art and activism known increasingly as *artivism* starts to get social as more artists see social tools as a way to reach more people and create greater social impact.

Examples Used: Artivist Film Festival and the Estria Foundation's Water Writes Project

2015 Trend Longevity Rating: B-

Art is still used frequently for activism and social media continues to amplify it, but this trend never accelerated beyond several interesting examples. Even today, there are examples of this same principle, but not enough to make this a top-rated trend.

12. Civic Engagement 2.0

A growing range of digital tools allows people to engage more actively with local governments on everything from reporting potholes to offering suggestions for improving their communities.

Examples Used: CitySourced and Give a Minute

2015 Trend Longevity Rating: B+

Though civic engagement hasn't quadrupled year after year, these tools to allow for deeper citizen engagement continue to grow and be adopted by more and more people. Though there hasn't yet been mass consolidation or a tipping point in usage, a growing number of tech-savvy cities are leading the way to help this trend continue to accelerate into the mainstream.

13. Tagging Reality

Better-quality mobile cameras allow developers to create tools that can tag any object in reality to unlock interactive content.

Examples Used: Layar and Sony SmartAR

2015 Trend Longevity Rating: C

This was a perfect example of the type of trend that may have been better explored as an element of a broader trend. Alone, it described a few isolated efforts, but over the course of several years, the trend never quite accelerated as quickly as I first described.

14. ChangeSourcing

Crowdsourcing itself is evolving beyond information sharing to a point where people can use the collaborative power of the crowd to achieve personal, social or political change.

Examples Used: Self-reported clinical trials and Peerbackers.com

2015 Trend Longevity Rating: B

The basic idea behind this trend was focused on how crowdsourcing was moving beyond information and into action as people tapped the power of crowds to achieve real things. This trend continued with multiple new sites and efforts using it in past few years.

15. Retail Theater

In the coming year, more retail stores will create unique experiences using the principles of theater to engage customers with memorable experiences.

Examples Used: Puma Creative Factory and Villa Sofa

2015 Trend Longevity Rating: A

Over the past several years, retailers have tried to get even more theatrical to combat the dangers of showrooming and the rise of online retail. If anything, this is making retail experiences even more interactive and dramatic than before.

Want to Read the Full Report for Free?

Visit www.15trends.com to read and download the full report.

APPENDIX C: 2013 Trends

THE BACKSTORY

In the third year of producing the trend report, the level of detail exploded as the full report went from about 20 pages to more than 100. The report featured more examples, more analysis—and more trends (with 3 bonus trends added to the usual 15).

The report was still delivered primarily in a visual presentation format, but this year there was an accompanying ebook available for sale on Amazon featuring not only the trends, but also suggestions on how to put them into action.

This third edition ebook was an immediate best seller on Amazon, remaining the number-one book in the market research category for eight straight weeks after launch and has been viewed more than 200,000 times online. The clean visuals, level of detail and growing reputation for the annual report resulted in plenty of sharing and comments online as well.

RETROSPECTIVE – HOW ACCURATE WAS THIS REPORT?

Developing the trends for 2013 was a more deliberate process requiring more research and a higher standard of proof before including any particular trend in the report. Topics featured in the 2013 report included the future of print publishing, the rise of women in business, authenticity in the banking sector, hyper-local commerce and the evolution of the travel industry. From these, there were several that received my own top longevity rating two years later as being early to predict large shifts in marketing and business.

THE 2013 TRENDS: RECAP & ANALYSIS

1. ## Shoptimization

   New mobile apps and startups let consumers optimize the process of buying everything from fashion to medical prescriptions.

   Examples Used: Slice, Dashlane, ShopSavvy, GoodRx, Rent the Runway, Wish Want Wear, Le Tote, CardStar, Perx, Keyring and Macy's in-store GPS

   2015 Trend Longevity Rating: A

   Thanks to increasing competition among retailers and a rising tide of new productivity tools online, the task of optimizing each of our shopping experiences has continued to be a top priority for all types of brands.

2. ## Partnership Publishing

   Aspiring authors and publishing professionals team up to create a new do-it-together models of publishing.

   Examples Used: Net Minds, Mindvalley, Paper Lantern Lit, and The Domino Project

   2015 Trend Longevity Rating: B+

   While the attention on these types of high-profile partnerships in the publishing industry has dissipated somewhat, this do-it-together approach to continues to accelerate as the entire industry maintains its rapid pace of innovation.

3. ## Human Banking

   Aiming to change years of growing distrust, banks finally uncover their human side by taking a more simple and direct approach to services and communication

   Examples Used: Ally Bank, FoundersCard, Zuno Bank, the IRS form redesign, Simple, BillGuard, and Project Catalyst

   2015 Trend Longevity Rating: A

Every new financial crisis underscores the importance of more human interactions between us and our financial institutions. Continued consumer distrust of the entire industry means that more banks and financial services groups will be considering how to use this trend in 2015.

4. MeFunding

Crowdfunding evolves beyond films or budding entrepreneurs to offer anyone the opportunity to seek financial support to do anything from taking a life-changing trip to paying for a college education.

Examples Used: Upstart, GoFundMe, GiveForward, Takeashine, Give-College and Indiegogo

2015 Trend Longevity Rating: B-

While the many sites featured as part of this trend remain available for people to use, the trend didn't quite explode in the way I predicted. This is one of those ideas that sees a steady stream of attention and usage but has not yet accelerated beyond that.

5. Powered by Women

Business leaders, pop culture and groundbreaking new research intersect to prove that our ideal future will be led by women.

Examples Used: *The Athena Doctrine* by John Gerzema and Michael D'Antonio, The Girl Effect, Girls Who Code, WIT, *Fast Company's* Influential Women In Technology list, *Brave* the movie, *The Hunger Games* movies, *Twilight* movies and *Revolution* TV series

2015 Trend Longevity Rating: A

There is no denying the role of women in business, culture and politics has grown year after year. Today there are more female leaders, role models and celebrated citizens than ever before—and it is a wonderful thing. This is one of those world-changing trends that we should all hope continues to accelerate every year.

6. Method Consulting

Successful entrepreneurs and companies create on-the-side consulting models to help others duplicate their success.

Examples Used: The Disney Institute, Zappos Insights, Sales Lion and Mindvalley Insights

2015 Trend Longevity Rating: B

The hunger for companies to learn from one another continues to be a big topic, however this trend predicted a huge growth in this type of consulting practice, and it hasn't really materialized on the scale I predicted. There are still big notable examples of it, but they are mostly the same as the ones shared in this report, with few proven additions.

7. Precious Print

Thanks to our digital-everything culture, the few objects and moments we choose to interact with in print become more valuable.

Examples Used: Esopus, Monocle, *NewsWeek*, Paper Because, Moo Luxe cards, *Star Trek Federation: The First 150 Years* by David Goodman, Moleskine notebooks, Wantful

2015 Trend Longevity Rating: A

As digital tools and interfaces get nicer and nicer, more experiences are moving to the digital sphere and fewer remain in print. Even so, the basic human behavior outlined in this trend—that we place even more value on the things that are printed because they are so much more rare—continues year after year.

8. Backstorytelling

Organizations discover that one of their greatest assets to inspire loyalty can come from taking people behind the scenes of their brand and history.

Examples Used: Land Rover, Ford, CustomInk and McDonald's Canada's Our Food. Your Questions website

2015 Trend Longevity Rating: A

As social platforms splinter but also grow in popularity, the necessity for brands to share their backstory in multiple ways continues to grow. Add this to the rising consciousness of consumers about the ethical business practices of companies and this trend has a perfect storm to continue to matter in 2015.

9. Social Visualization

Going beyond data, new tools and technologies to let people include visualizations as part of their social profiles and conversations online.

Examples Used: The new MySpace, Infusd, Coca-Cola's new website and Cowbird

2015 Trend Longevity Rating: A

Visual interfaces continue to be commonplace and popular. In fact, if anything – this trend has grown so fast that it no longer really qualifies as "non-obvious." Its popularity and growth, however, gave it a top rating in this recap.

10. Healthy Content

Healthcare organizations feel pressure to create more useful and substantial health content to satisfy increasingly empowered patients who have become unreachable through pure marketing or advertising messages.

Examples Used: Diabetapedia, the CDC's response to the year's meningitis scare, the Cleveland Clinic's Health Hub and Boehringer Ingelheim teaming up with PSFK

2015 Trend Longevity Rating: B+

In the healthcare industry, content continues to be golden because empowered patients gain more confidence and increasingly turn to the web before seeking information from other sources.

11. Degree-Free Learning

Quality of e-learning content explodes as more students consider alternatives to traditional college educations.

Examples Used: CreativeLive, Uncollege, [E]nstitute, Fluent in 3 Months and Soundslice

2015 Trend Longevity Rating: B+

Learning and higher education are simultaneously changed by this growth of people who choose to learn new skills and industries without requiring a degree to display at the end of it. While this has not overtaken traditional degree-granting programs, it continues to gain in popularity.

12. Friend-Sourced Travel

New and old friends change the travel experience by curating where to go and offering more authentic local experiences.

Examples Used: Vayable, Dine with the Dutch, SupperKing, Trippy, Airbnb and TripBirds

2015 Trend Longevity Rating: B-

At some level, this has always happened through social media platforms. This trend prediction was focused on the belief that there would be far more platforms to enable this type of engagement, which didn't really take off in subsequent years.

13. MicroInnovation

Thinking small becomes the new competitive advantage as slight changes to features or benefits create big value.

Examples Used: Toyota Easy-Fill tire alert, Mercedes-Benz Magic Vision wipers, Ford Liftgate, Apple iPod and Universal Lubricants

2015 Trend Longevity Rating: A

If anything, this trend has accelerated dramatically in recent years as more brands adopt a lean startup mentality that encourages them to make incremental changes to products in ways that can deliver big value.

14. Hyper-Local Commerce

New services and technology make it easier for anyone to invest in local businesses and buy from local merchants.

Examples Used: Square, GoPayment, MobilePay, Paypal Here, Shopify, Popularise, Fundrise, Goodzer, Sears Local and Peixe Urbano

2015 Trend Longevity Rating: A

Whether you examine this trend in relation to the growth of local commerce or as fueled by investment and interest in mobile commerce platforms and experience, the fact is consumer experiences continue to become more local and focused on customization and personalization from brands of all sizes. This trend is likely to continue.

15. Heroic Design

Design takes a leading role in the introduction of new products, ideas and campaigns to change the world.

Examples Used: Stanford Design for Change Center, Project H Design, Kony2012, LifeStraw, Information Blanket, ChangeMakers ColaLife and "The Wire" from Frog Design

2015 Trend Longevity Rating: A

Thanks to an intersection between this trend and increased crowdfunding, ideas for heroic design products can not only be funded and supported online, but they also have increasing opportunities for media exposure in a consumer world more engaged with and hungry for amazing business stories.

16. Bonus Trend: Branded Inspiration

Brands use awe-inspiring moments, innovative ideas and dramatic stunts to capture attention and demonstrate their values to the world.

Examples Used: RedBull Stratos, Toyota 100 Cars for Good and Nature Valley Trailview

2015 Trend Longevity Rating: B+

While 2013 was a watershed year for brands to use big moments for inspiration, the trend continued with large investments into social movements from brands like Dove, and social experimentation in bringing people together, like efforts from Coca-Cola.

17. Bonus Trend: Optimistic Aging

A wealth of content online and new social networks inspire people of all ages to feel more optimistic about getting older.

Examples Used: YourEncore and Intent

2015 Trend Longevity Rating: A

When it comes to aging, there are more reasons for optimism than ever. Technology gets better at offering mobility and predictive interfaces, while overall health services and living options continue to improve.

18. Bonus Trend: Audio Tagging

Audio is used by brands as a doorway to unlock more content, create engagement or drive consumer behavior.

Examples Used: IBM and Shazam, Into_Now from Yahoo! and Elias Arts

2015 Trend Longevity Rating: C

This was a perfect example of an overly optimistic trend based on a nascent concept that hasn't quite broken into the mainstream.

Want to Read the Full Report for Free?

Visit www.15trends.com to read and download the full report.

APPENDIX D: 2014 Trends

THE BACKSTORY

This fourth edition of the *Non-Obvious Trend Report* was expanded in several ways from previous reports. The first and most visible change was that the report now featured five categories for trends instead of simply listing 15 in random order. The categories are the same as those used in the 2015 report.

In addition, the report featured deeper examples, more actionable advice and a new visual look that spotlighted each trend more deeply and encouraged people to learn more about each one. The overall report was more than 160 pages.

In an effort to build visibility, in 2014 I also made the vast majority of the report freely available online rather than moving it to an ebook available for sale on Amazon. The result was wider distribution of the report, and far lower sales of the corresponding ebook.

RETROSPECTIVE – HOW ACCURATE WAS THIS REPORT?

Given that this report is only a year old, almost every trend is still applicable to business today. As a result, I was tempted not to go through the process of rating each trend because the time since they were published is so short, but I still think there is value in reviewing them, so you will find the same analysis of the 2014 trends in the following pages.

THE 2014 TRENDS: RECAP & ANALYSIS

1. **Desperate Detox (Culture & Consumer Behavior Trend)**

   Consumers try to more authentically connect with others and seek out moments of reflection by intentionally disconnecting from the technology surrounding them.

   Examples Used: Nomophobia, Camp Grounded, Human Mode app, *Fast Company*'s #unplug hashtag, Belize and FOMO

   2015 Trend Longevity Rating: A

   Technology is only becoming more omnipresent in our lives, making this trend one that continues to grow in 2015.

2. **Media Binging (Culture & Consumer Behavior Trend)**

   As more media and entertainment is available on any device on demand, consumers binge and are willing to pay extra for the convenience.

   Examples Used: Breaking Bad TV show, *Beyoncé* album release, Netflix, telecom data plans, *House of Cards* TV show and Pocket app

   2015 Trend Longevity Rating: A

   Streaming options continue to expand and consumer behavior follows, making this trend one to continue to watch in 2015.

3. **Obsessive Productivity (Culture & Consumer Behavior Trend)**

   With thousands of life-optimizing apps and instant advice from social media–savvy self-help gurus, becoming more productive has become the ultimate obsession.

   Examples Used: Narrative, Swiftkey, Manhattan Disney moms and Coffitivity

   2015 Trend Longevity Rating: A

   Last year brought plenty of new bestselling books talking about optimizing your life, hacking your daily chores and saving time. To say people continue to obsess over their own productivity is becoming an understatement.

4. **Subscription Commerce (Economics & Entrepreneurship Trend)**

More unexpected businesses and retailers use subscriptions to sell recurring services or products to customers instead of focusing on the one-time sale.

Examples Used: Adobe Creative Cloud, Amazon Prime, Oyster Books, Pleygo.com, Moviepass, Trunk Club, Bulu Box, Birchbox, Carnivore Club, Love with Food and Shoe Dazzle

2015 Trend Longevity Rating: B+

More industries and brands turn to the lessons of subscription commerce, but the more powerful effect of this trend will come from how subscription-based models that were launched in 2014 grow and receive more attention in 2015.

5. **Instant Entrepreneurs (Economics & Entrepreneurship Trend)**

Better support, incentives and tools mean anyone with an idea can launch a startup knowing that the costs and risks of failure are not as high as they once were.

Examples Used: LegalZoom, coworking spaces, Strikingly, Bitcoin mining, StockLogos.com and Startup America

2015 Trend Longevity Rating: A

The shift in many industries from full-time employee to entrepreneur continues to take shape as top professionals continue to branch out on their own.

6. **Collaborative Economy (Economics & Entrepreneurship Trend)**

New business models and tools allow consumers and brands to use sharing and collaborative consumption for new ways to buy, sell or consume almost anything.

Examples Used: Crowd Companies, Heineken Ideas Brewery, GE's partnership with Quirky and Patagonia's partnership with Ebay

2015 Trend Longevity Rating: A

While growing last year, the shared or collaborative economy has become one of the more obvious trends anyone could point to today, a symbol of its continued rapid acceleration.

7. Branded Utility (Marketing & Social Media Trend)

Brands use content marketing and greater integration between marketing and operations to augment promotions with real ways to add value to customer's lives.

Examples Used: Content Rules by Ann Handley and C. C. Chapman; *Ctrl Alt Delete* by Mitch Joel; *Jab, Jab, Jab, Right Hook* by Gary Vaynerchuk; *Weber's Way to Grill* by Jamie Purviance; Charmin's Sit or Squat website and KLM's Wanna Gives

2015 Trend Longevity Rating: A

As content marketing continues to dramatically change the way that marketers communicate with their audiences, there have been dozens more examples of brands using this trend across 2014.

8. Lovable Imperfection (Marketing & Social Media Trend)

Consumers seek out true authenticity and reward minor imperfections in products, personalities and brands by showing greater loyalty and trust.

Examples Used: Jennifer Lawrence, Domino's Artisan Pizza, McDonald's Egg White McMuffin, *Despicable Me* and MegaMind

2015 Trend Longevity Rating: A

The impact of this trend was so powerful in business across the year following its initial publication, that the 2015 trend of Unperfection relates directly to this one from 2014.

9. Shareable Humanity (Marketing & Social Media Trend)

Content shared on social media gets more emotional as people share amazing examples of humanity and brands inject more of it into communications efforts.

Examples Used: Mashable stories, Kikkoman and Hopemob,

2015 Trend Longevity Rating: B

This was one of the trends from the previous year that was negatively affected by the fatigue some media consumers are starting to experience from overly dramatic media stories and clickbaiting headlines. Regardless, we continue to find human stories irresistible to read and share.

10. Privacy Paranoia

New data breaches are leading to a new global sense of paranoia about what governments and brands know about us—and how they might use this big data in potentially harmful ways.

Examples Used: DuckDuckGo, Lendup.com, Cloaking, International Data Privacy Day and "The Deep Web" from *Time* magazine

2015 Trend Longevity Rating: B-

As more tools enter the market to help consumers protect their information and take back control of their privacy, this paranoia is shifting to empowerment.

11. Microdesign

As communication becomes more visual, design gains respect and integrates into business. Demand for design skills also explodes, leading to easier access to bite-sized chunks of design expertise.

Examples Used: Candy Crush, Infogr.am, Visual.ly, PicktoChart, *Microinteractions* by Dan Saffer, Swiftly and Over app

2015 Trend Longevity Rating: A

The need for design expertise in every corner of business continues to grow, and this trend is still an important one for any type of organization to consider.

12. Overquantified Life

As big data leads brands to overload data with cute infographics and superficial analysis, they add more confusion about what all this data really means, and how it can inform decisions in real life.

Examples Used: Kred, Klout, Jawbone, Fitbit and Google Glass

2015 Trend Longevity Rating: B

Connecting all the data we collect on ourselves in a meaningful way continues to be a challenge, however, consumers are feeling less overquantified and more in control of this data.

13. Curated Sensationalism

As the line between news and entertainment blurs, smart curation displaces journalism as content is paired with sensational headlines to drive millions of views.

Examples Used: Buzzfeed, Upworthy, *Forbes*, ThunderClap and SunnySkyz

2015 Trend Longevity Rating: A

Media continues to deliver over-the-top headlines and sensationalism that continue to negatively affect consumer trust in media.

14. Distributed Expertise

The idea of expertise itself shifts to become more inclusive, less academic and more widely available on demand and in real time.

Examples Used: Plated, Contently, Vikram Patel, Kaggle, Pop Expert and Clarity.fm

2015 Trend Longevity Rating: A

Learning through experts online in many formats is still a big trend and one that is powering some of the fastest growing learning platforms online today (including many profiled in this original trend).

15. Anti-Stereotyping

Across media and entertainment, traditional gender roles are being reversed, assumptions about alternative lifestyles are being challenged and perceptions of what defines anyone evolve in new ways.

Examples Used: "Lean Out" from *Bloomberg Businessweek*, Hasbro Easy Bake Oven, *In A World ...* the movie, the Bic for Her pen firestorm, Tide laundry, *Delusions of Gender* by Cordelia Fine, *A Call to Action* by Jimmy Carter and *Whistling Vivaldi* by Claude Steele

2015 Trend Longevity Rating: A

The reversing of gender roles continues to be a big opportunity for brands to get their messaging right, or wrong, when it comes to speaking to these diverse groups through marketing and communications.

Want to Read the Full Report for Free?

Visit www.15trends.com to read and download the full report.

INDEX